23'-

THE
SKEPTICAL
INVESTOR

John Lawrence Reynolds

The SKEPTICAL Investor

How to Grow and Protect Your Retirement Savings

VIKING
CANADA

VIKING CANADA

Published by the Penguin Group

Penguin Group (Canada), 90 Eglinton Avenue East, Suite 700,
Toronto, Ontario, Canada M4P 2Y3 (a division of Pearson Canada Inc.)

Penguin Group (USA) Inc., 375 Hudson Street, New York, New York 10014, U.S.A.
Penguin Books Ltd, 80 Strand, London WC2R 0RL, England
Penguin Ireland, 25 St Stephen's Green, Dublin 2, Ireland
(a division of Penguin Books Ltd)
Penguin Group (Australia), 250 Camberwell Road, Camberwell, Victoria 3124, Australia
(a division of Pearson Australia Group Pty Ltd)
Penguin Books India Pvt Ltd, 11 Community Centre, Panchsheel Park,
New Delhi – 110 017, India
Penguin Group (NZ), 67 Apollo Drive, Rosedale, North Shore 0632, New Zealand
(a division of Pearson New Zealand Ltd)
Penguin Books (South Africa) (Pty) Ltd, 24 Sturdee Avenue, Rosebank,
Johannesburg 2196, South Africa

Penguin Books Ltd, Registered Offices: 80 Strand, London WC2R 0RL, England

First published 2010

1 2 3 4 5 6 7 8 9 10   (RRD)

Copyright © John Lawrence Reynolds, 2010

Author representation: Westwood Creative Artists
94 Harbord Street, Toronto, Ontario M5S 1G6

Manufactured in the U.S.A.

LIBRARY AND ARCHIVES CANADA CATALOGUING IN PUBLICATION
Reynolds, John Lawrence
The skeptical investor : how to grow and protect your retirement savings / John Lawrence
Reynolds.
Includes bibliographical references and index.
ISBN 978-0-670-06405-2
1. Retirement income—Planning. 2. Portfolio management. 3. Registered Retirement
Savings Plans. 4. Finance, Personal. I. Title.
HG179.R492 2010   332.024'0145   C2009-906286-0

Visit the website of John Lawrence Reynolds at **www.wryter.ca**
Visit the Penguin Group (Canada) website at **www.penguin.ca**
Special and corporate bulk purchase rates available; please see
www.penguin.ca/corporatesales or call 1-800-810-3104, ext. 2477 or 2474

FOR HILARY,
WITH GRATITUDE AND CHOCOLATE

It is easier to make money than to save it.
One is exertion. The other is self-denial.

—THOMAS CHANDLER HALIBURTON

Listen, when a man makes money
he has to keep two steps in front of the people
trying to take it from him. You find it. They take it.

—SIR HARRY OAKES

CONTENTS

INTRODUCTION

Life is hazardous. Survive the challenges of childhood and you enter adolescence, an endless flood of risks involving illegal substances and immoral temptations. Emerge from there to encounter uncertainty in your job and relationships, perhaps eventually adding the responsibility of protecting your own kids from the risks you managed to navigate around, if you were fortunate.

Then, as though compensating for the anticipated selective dysfunction of old age, the warm glow of retirement looms on the horizon, much of it funded by registered retirement savings plan (RRSP) contributions. It's the end of the rainbow, a pot of gold unguarded by leprechauns and unsullied with the guilt of government handouts. It bears your name. It's yours to spend. And when you step away from your job for the final time, it will be waiting for you.

You hope.

These days, projected pension benefits are as common as 10-cent beer and 50-cent pantyhose. Set aside those dreams of sailing the Mediterranean in June and walking warm beaches in January for a moment. Step over here and meet Retirement Reality, a slobbering beast with hairy earlobes, handing out debits for savings accounts, a nasty monster showing up on the doorsteps of too many ready-to-retire Canadians.

The Pension Plan You Always Wanted Is the One Others Are Enjoying

A generation ago, virtually all employers offered their workers a pension plan, usually promising defined benefits. This kind of plan determined a fixed amount paid each year through your retirement, employing a formula based on your income. Typically, your retirement income would represent 70 percent of the earnings you received during your final five years of work. Having shed many expenses of your working years, such as mortgage payments, commuting costs, your kids' budgets, and other drains on your income, and qualifying for various tax breaks and government handouts to be added to your bank account, this was likely to be an adequate amount. With a little planning, you could anticipate a lifestyle close to the one you had when you were rising with the sun each morning, gnashing your teeth at the boss all day, and dreaming about retirement at night.

Defined-benefit pensions were a product of the Age of Innocence—meaning pre-1980, when large corporations such as Northern Telecom (Nortel), Massey-Ferguson, General Motors, Canadian Pacific, and others were expected to keep operating forever, or at least over the lifetimes of their pensioned employees.

My, how things have changed. Many of those companies have vanished; the rest are feeble and struggling. And while the corporations promising the defined-benefit pensions are becoming extinct, the rest of us are living far longer than the designers of those old-style pensions expected. What was once reasonable for companies to provide for their retirees now appears impossible because the nest egg is being tapped longer than planned. To make things worse, many of the companies that are committed to these plans, if they're still around, employ fewer people to generate the profits needed to keep the money flowing. General Motors, it's rumoured, has five retirees receiving pensions for every worker building its cars, explaining one of several reasons why automotive companies have practically run off the road entirely.

Couldn't the actuaries who plot this kind of stuff see the problem coming? Apparently not. Nor could the unions, which kept pushing for defined-benefit pensions. During periods when companies were generating surpluses in their pension assets, union leaders demanded that benefits be raised to match the increase, yet when things turned sour, the unions insisted that benefits not be reduced.

Even fortunate Canadians who remain employed by firms offering defined-benefit plans have been shaken by the credit crisis. Domtar's pension managers, for example, purchased $445 million in Asset-Backed Commercial Paper (ABCP) in 2006–2007, much of it based on the sub-prime mortgages that triggered the sinking of the global economy in 2008–2009. These investments represented a whopping 30 percent of the total pension fund assets recorded at the end of 2007. By February 2009, Domtar's pension fund had written off almost $200 million, suggesting the company will have to lower pension payments and raise employee contributions to honour its commitment to retirees.*

This is not an unusual situation. At the beginning of 2008, Canadian companies with defined-benefit plans reportedly had sufficient cash to cover 96 percent of their pension obligations— money that would be available even if the companies declared bankruptcy. One year later, these same firms harboured less than 70 percent of the money needed to cover the same obligations.†

Companies that are still around and solvent avoid defined-benefit plans, where employees are told, "Here's what you get when you leave." They have switched to defined-*contribution* plans, where retirees are basically advised, "Work it out on your own and remember to close the door when you leave"—the only way for

---

*Canadian Centre for Ethics and Corporate Policy, *The Canadian Asset-Backed Commercial Paper Crisis*, March 26, 2009, p. 12.
†Kristine Owram, The Canadian Press, *Struggling Pension Plans Call on Government to Relax Funding Rules*, January 11, 2009.

employers to avoid the long-term obligations of defined-benefit programs that, in the private sector, are a dying breed.

Working Seven Years Longer before Saying "Adios!"

About the only workers enjoying defined-benefit pension plans these days are government employees, who glide from the womb of public-service job security to the warm lap of a lifelong income that reflects salary levels achieved during their years of highest earnings. Unlike almost all workers in the private sector, public-service employees don't mess around with the Retirement Lottery, hoping to make the correct investment decisions and aiming for some unpredictable asset level when they retire. It's there for them to collect when they end their working years: a fixed amount linked to their working income, making the transition from labourer to loafer as smooth as stepping off an escalator.

While you're grumbling over that fact because you're self-employed or work for a company with defined-contribution pensions, chew on this: A 2008 Treasury Board study determined that federal public servants in Canada pay a mere 28 percent of the service costs to manage their pension plans. You, however, pay 100 percent of the same cost while picking up almost three-quarters of the expense of ensuring those other people receive the benefits to which they're entitled.

If you are employed in the federal public service, your retirement savings are protected behind a high and impregnable wall and your income is predetermined and guaranteed, so you may feel you don't need this book. You're welcome, however, to stick around and see how the rest of us need to build and protect our retirement savings. Of course, if you have investments outside a pension plan, either registered within an RRSP or registered retirement income fund (RRIF), you'll find plenty of valuable information to safeguard your portfolio on the following pages. This book is specifically directed, however, at the many

Canadians who, when it comes to retirement income planning, are like the first little pig in the fairy tale, huddling within a house of straw that may collapse with the first strong puff from a passing wolf.

Knowing how Canadians employed in the public service enjoy a defined-benefit pension plan, are you surprised to learn they retire at the average age of 59—versus the rest of us, who typically work until we're 66 years old? Wouldn't you like an extra seven years of a guaranteed income to cover your green fees, travel costs, and hammocks?

The Risk Is All Yours. But the Profits Aren't.

Think of comfortable retirement as a vacation destination, a place to enjoy walks on the beach, play some afternoon golf, do a little fishing, find time for a little card playing, and sample a whole bunch of relaxation. Now: How do you get there?

People with traditional defined-benefit pensions let others do the driving. They rarely worry about bad weather, detours, toll roads, and other travel hazards, which are the concern of whoever is sitting up front and doing the driving. Defined-benefit pension people travel the route to retirement unconcerned about trading costs, rates of return, and asset allocation, not to mention greedy financial advisors and fraud artists.

You, however, are behind the wheel of your own pension plan, probably an RRSP. You can hire a chauffeur to choose the route and speed, avoid the bumps, and drive you safely to your destination, but chauffeurs cost money. You could drive yourself, except you don't know the route. Even more serious, you probably don't know how to drive.

This travel analogy is simplified but appropriate because more of us are finding ourselves in charge of something we don't know how to operate—in this case, a complex, long-term investment. The knowledge quotient varies, but it remains abysmally low.

Before the credit crisis of 2008–2009, the asset values of some RRSPs exceeded $1 million, yet many of their owners had no idea how to define a mutual fund, how to measure (or even define) a management expense ratio (MER),* how to handle asset allocation, and how to protect themselves against a repeat of the severe collapse suffered by their portfolios in 2008 and 2009.

These were the lucky ones. They employed qualified financial guides and earned enough income to make substantial contributions to the plan over several years. Of course, a million dollars doesn't buy all that it used to, but all those zeros in their accounts make retirement a little more fun and a lot less worrisome. Permit me, however, to ask three totally valid, and somewhat cynical, questions:

1 *How much more could they have accrued over the same period, making the same contributions, if they had cut their investment expenses by even 1 percent annually?* Losing 2 or 3 percent each passing year to excessive fees may not sound like much, but over time it can reduce the potential growth of an RRSP by half. Which would you rather have in your RRSP account when you retire—$1 million or $2 million?

2 *How much did these holders of $1 million RRSPs lose to incompetent or self-interested advice from sources more interested in lining their own pockets than in building their clients' assets?* Perhaps 90 percent of all RRSP/RRIF transactions are conducted by licensed professionals whose income level is determined almost exclusively by the commissions earned from those same transactions. Other professions use the same method of remuneration, of course. Like used-car salespeople.

---

*The management expense ratio (MER) is the amount of money expressed as a percentage of the mutual fund's total assets, removed from the fund annually as the management fee.

3 *How well were these RRSP investors protected against*
   catastrophic losses during the credit crisis of 2008–2009?
   RRSP owners need to shield their savings against losses as
   they approach retirement age. A simple, easy-to-implement
   technique can be applied to create this protection, but few
   advisors employ it.

This last point represents one of the most unassailable criticisms
of the investment industry, in my opinion. Comprising brokers,
financial advisors, mutual fund salespeople, and countless behind-
the-scenes individuals and corporations, the investment industry
promotes itself as dedicated to helping clients reach their financial
and investment goals. In the case of RRSP and many Tax-Free
Savings Account (TFSA) investors, this means both building and
protecting their assets over the long term.

The protection aspect is critical (and the basis of this book)
because the performance of stocks and bonds varies widely.
Or, as advisors frequently shrug when clients complain about
substantial losses in their account: "The markets go up and the
markets go down."

Precisely. Unfortunately, too many financial advisors respond
to this axiom like dogs on a Ferris wheel, wagging their tales
in ecstasy as things rise and grabbing a quick nap as they
descend.

It is nonsense for anyone in the industry to plead ignorance
("We didn't see it coming!") about the emergence of a bear
market, including the one that savaged the assets of RRSP investors
in 2008–2009. Did they, as investment professionals, honestly
believe markets relentlessly rise toward infinity? Every licensed
securities advisor knows that markets ebb and flow. The amplitude
and schedule of cycles may be indeterminate, but they occur as
surely as the passage of the sun across the sky each day. Too many
advisors are driven by a system that encourages investors to

purchase and hold expensive mutual funds, generating fat commissions and fees for advisors while returning unimpressive earnings for investors.

The commission-based remuneration system for advisors remains at the heart of most investor concerns. Think of it for a moment: Would you entrust your health to a physician whose income was earned from commissions on the pharmaceuticals he or she prescribed for you?

A few financial advisors will (and already have, based on responses to previous books) cry that I'm being unfair about their livelihood. They fail to receive reasonable credit for building portfolios when markets are rising, they'll whine, but everyone is prepared to jump on them when losses occur. "Clients don't complain when their accounts are rising in value, only when they fall!" they grumble. Which is like saying a leaky roof is fine on a sunny day because it only needs to work when rain falls. A roof's primary purpose is to protect the resident against the elements. And a financial advisor's role is to see that the investment fund grows, not shrinks, over time.

The advisor complaints are specious. More than that, they are insulting. During the bull market of 2003 to 2006, a dart-throwing monkey could have picked stocks and mutual funds that made money. Canadians investing for their retirement years need more than someone who collects commissions and fees when the markets soar; they need someone who truly gives a damn when the markets plunge, as markets inevitably do from time to time.

Investors suffer a severe disconnect between their concept of a financial advisor's role and the industry's actions. The vast majority of Canadians expect financial advisors to play the role of fiduciary, a heavyweight term meaning someone who holds someone else's property in trust. "In trust" connotes not merely having possession of a property but caring for it to the benefit of its actual owner. Yet the industry, regardless of its protestations through various channels, regards advisors as merely licensed salespersons, and fights with tooth and nail any claim that its actions involve a fiduciary role.

Everyone who relies upon services rewarded via commissions or fees to a financial advisor has an expectation that their advisor will pay as much attention to the preservation of capital as to its acquisition. When the investor's age is 50-plus years and the portfolio's value is in six figures, it should be more than an expectation: It should be an unchallenged right.

Advice based on an advisor's self-interest or derived from outright incompetence is the most common cause of unnecessary investor losses, but other disasters can occur, of course. Like fraud, embezzlement, and theft.

Bank Robbery Is Hard Work Compared with Investment Fraud

With absolutely no intention of planting larcenous ideas in your mind, here's something you should know: *The easiest way to get your hands on other people's money with the least chance of being caught, and even less chance of receiving a long jail term, is through investment fraud aimed at RRSP owners who are 50 or older.*

White-collar crime in Canada often appears to be treated as a victimless event by our courts and justice system. Theft that would slap you in a grey-bar hotel for 20 or 30 years if committed in the United States usually earns you a few months in a minimum-security establishment in Canada. If it's your first offence and no physical injury was inflicted, your incarceration period is reduced by five-sixths. Which means that if you receive a six-year sentence for your crimes, you'll spend a year playing chess and watching TV before being back on the street—initially in a halfway house for a few months and eventually regaling your buddies at the neighbourhood bar with tales of life in the big house. Assuming, of course, that your buddies do not include the people you defrauded in the first place.

Exaggeration? Consider these examples:

BRE-X. One of the world's largest mining scandals, the Bre-X fraud robbed trusting investors of an estimated $300 million. After an investigation extending for more than two years, not one criminal charge was laid. The Ontario Securities Commission brought charges of insider trading against a single key player in 2001. Six years later, without even making an appearance in court, this sole defendant was acquitted.

IAN THOW. The senior vice-president of Berkshire Investments flew his private corporate jet around the world, drank 100-year-old Scotch whisky at $10,000 per bottle, and flaunted the high life to Canadians who entrusted him with their money. He lived in luxury near Portland, Oregon, while his former clients, many of whom alleged that their retirement savings had been wiped out, fumed for years. Thow was arrested in February 2009 and charged with defrauding clients of $32 million.

DAVID BLOW. Convicted of fraud from a previous scheme, Blow convinced members of his church congregation to invest $6.5 million of their retirement funds with him. None of the money was recovered. Despite his record, Blow received a sentence of three and a half years in prison and was released after serving eight months.

SALIM DAMJI. Damji defrauded Islamic communities in Canada and elsewhere of as much as $100 million, spending all but $5 million of it on gambling and bad investments. Sentenced to seven and a half years in prison, Damji astonished his victims less than 18 months later when he strolled casually

among them in his old Toronto neighbourhood, released on
day parole.

EARL JONES. Jones was arrested in July 2009 and charged
with multiple counts of fraud and theft totalling as much as
$50 million, money that had been entrusted to him by
150 investors. Many of his clients were elderly residents of
nursing homes and hospitals. Jones and his wife, according
to investigators, lived well while it lasted, burning their way
through $50,000 of investors' money each month. The only
surprise in this tale is that Jones was allegedly never licensed
by the province of Quebec. He called himself a financial
advisor and people believed him.

These scoundrels and others like them prey on their victims' trust,
something that people older than 50 years of age tend to possess
in greater amounts than the younger set. Lacking the cynicism of
Generation X, older folk trust that another person's word is their
bond and want to believe that everyone maintains the same high
moral standard as their own. Once they have built a nest egg over
30 or 40 years of work, they cannot believe that someone they
trust will walk away with it. When this happens, the victims expect
a) to recover their losses, and b) to see the perpetrators pay for
their crimes with punishment that includes several years behind
bars. That would be fair; sadly, fair is rare.

And Then, Of Course, There's the Odd Global Economic Meltdown
Even if you manage to make good investment decisions, minimize
costs associated with your portfolio, and avoid jackals determined
to snack on your hard-earned retirement savings, you cannot avoid
feeling the force of financial disasters such as the one that shook
the world's confidence in late 2008.

Periodic slides in stock-market values are known as *corrections*, a term that recalls images of a teacher marking your grade four spelling test. Every couple of decades, something akin to the most recent calamity occurs despite assurances that all is well—the claim supported by assurances that "The economy is in great shape!" and "Things have never been better!" usually uttered by smiling politicians.*

You may have watched the innards of your own RRSP, RRIF, or TFSA portfolio being ripped to shreds by the 2008–2009 event known variously as the Great Recession, the New Depression, the Credit Crisis, and the "What-the-hell-happened?" incident. Since about 1990, while you were diligently adding to your retirement savings portfolio through the fruits of your daily labour, other folks were earning multi-million-dollar salaries and bonuses by selling financial sows' ears as investment silk purses.

Here are two things to count on: The financial conjurors behind those shenanigans are not at all worried about damage to *their* retirement nest eggs, unless it means cutting back on the number of yachts they plan to own; and similar events of varying scope and origin will occur again in coming years, each of them deflating the value of your retirement savings.

The closer you move toward retirement, the more harrowing these disruptions become. Grumbling about the unfairness of market manipulators, charlatans, and fraud artists will do nothing to restore your assets, and by the time your portfolio feels the impact of their hijinks, the damage will have been done.

Unless your entire RRSP or RRIF is in savings accounts under the protection of the Canada Deposit Insurance Corporation (CDIC), with each account totalling less than $100,000, do not expect anyone to replace losses suffered as a result of actions committed by others, whether they are brokers who "churn" (create excess buying and selling activity) your account to build commissions,

---

*For my take on the 2008 credit crisis, check out *Bubbles, Bankers & Bailouts* (D&M Publishers, 2009).

advisors who funnel your funds into pipelines leading to their own pockets, or sociopathic embezzlers who prey on your misplaced trust. You may, with time, recover a portion of your losses via civil and criminal action against such malfeasance. You may also win this weekend's lottery. Counting on either is like planting onions in the fall and hoping for tulips in the spring.

The Best Way to Deal with Unfairness, Ill Fortune, and Poor Timing Is to Prepare for Them

Among the most hallowed rules for Canadian RRSP investors over several years was the maxim *buy and hold*, carved into granite by gurus such as Warren Buffett. The system was simple to follow, if somewhat more difficult to execute: Buy shares in quality companies. Ignore fluctuations in stock prices, international crises, bonds and GICs, technological innovations, and unfolding events. Hold them until either you or your heirs need the money. Just get into the market carefully and stay there.

Investors who heeded this advice at the beginning of the new millennium have a right to assume that Buffett and his disciples have all the investment acumen of tree stumps. See for yourself:

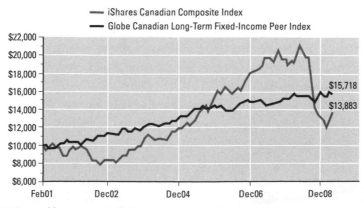

iShares Canadian Composite Index
Globe Canadian Long-Term Fixed-Income Peer Index

$15,718
$13,883

SOURCE: www.globeinvestor.com. Used with permission.

The dark line traces returns over the period from February 2001 to May 2009, comparing the performance of a popular exchange traded fund* with that of long-term bonds over the same period. While the three-year period from June 2005 to June 2008 delivered spectacular returns, that's only one-third of the period in question; for two-thirds of the time, you would have earned more from boring long-term bonds, the basis of the Long-Term Fixed Income Peer Index. Bonds are not the equities favoured by Buffett and most financial advisors. Bonds issued by federal and provincial governments in Canada are guaranteed; what you see on the paper is what you get paid on a fixed date.

Buy-and-hold proponents will note that shifting the time period a few months either way would show a different picture, likely favouring stocks. They would be correct. But faced with a fixed date, such as retirement, you lack the ability to do broad time-shifting. More to the point, this negates to at least some degree the near-universal faith in buy and hold as the ultimate investing philosophy. The closer you move toward retirement, the less you can tolerate the wild swing in stock prices known as *volatility*. Volatility in your RRSP is like the wilder escapades of your youth. Back then, you could tolerate it. In middle age and beyond, you should avoid it.

This book was prepared to assist you in equipping your investment portfolio with protection against attacks on your savings that are likely, or at least possible, including excessive volatility, inflation, high commissions and fees, outright fraud, and various other avoidable risks.

The techniques and suggestions provided here function similarly to the seatbelts and airbags in your car: They may not ensure that you escape injury entirely, but they sure improve your chances of survival.

---

*For definitions of exchange traded funds and other investment terms, please consult the Glossary on page 179.

I

WHAT THE HECK HAPPENED ANYWAY?

"It seems to me that a financial advisor should be as good at telling you when to get out of the market as telling you when to get in."

Suzanne Soucie smiles a little unconvincingly in the sunny living room of her suburban Toronto home. In her mid-60s, she retains much of her youthful beauty and optimistic outlook, but it's tinged with shadows of anger and regret.

She and her husband maintain separate RRSP accounts and, while each consults with the other about investment strategies, they make their own decisions and, in fact, have separate advisors in different bank-owned brokerages.

In 2001, fed up with the poor performance and high fees of the mutual funds in her $120,000 RRSP, she decided to move $70,000 of her equity investments into blue-chip stocks, leaving the balance in short-term government-backed strip bonds. Heeding her advisor's suggestion, she purchased shares in Royal Bank and TD Bank. "They were as blue-chip as you can get," she explains, "and I rolled the dividends into new share purchases."

It was a good move. By the summer of 2008, her shares had doubled in price, lifting her RRSP balance to more than $200,000.

"I figured whenever your investment rose that high, you should take some profits," Soucie recalls. "My husband keeps telling me, 'Nobody ever went broke taking profits,' and it made sense to sell at least half my bank shares and move the money into more bonds, just to solidify things."

When she proposed the idea to her advisor, however, the response was immediately negative.

"He almost begged me not to sell the bank shares," Soucie says, "saying that his firm had projected a target price about 10 percent higher for the bank stocks over the next year. He was really adamant and sincere. I mean, he wasn't making trailer fees or commissions off the shares, so he had nothing to lose if I sold. He just kept repeating the target price his company had for the banks, telling me there was no other way to be sure of making 10 percent in a year." She smiles and shakes her head. "So I held on to them. And a couple of weeks later, the slide began."

By the end of 2008, Soucie had lost almost all the profits she had made from the bank stocks. Assets that had taken almost seven years to build up vanished in less than six months.

"I know his advice was good in the beginning," she says, "and he wasn't trying to churn my account or put money in his own pocket. I just wish he understood that I wanted to start protecting the profits I had made because I'm going to be living off them within a few years, and you can't spend what isn't there."

Suzanne Soucie's financial advisor was hardly alone in missing the depth and breadth of the 2008 recession. Just a few months before the house of cards collapsed in September 2008, former U.S. Federal Reserve chairman Alan Greenspan was expressing confidence in the health and future growth of the American economy and, by extension, the world's. Which may explain part of the problem.

Other economists lacking Greenspan's celebrity, and independent financial advisors free to reach their own conclusions, recognized the warning signs long before the economic collapse. The clues were there to be read by anyone who chose to look at them: Waves of residential home foreclosures signalling the end of the housing boom were linked with tens of billions of dollars in liabilities based on mortgages for homes, stock prices were being manipulated, and hollowed-out securities were tagged as Asset-Backed Commercial Paper (ABCP) before being peddled around the world.

Things went over the top when cranks like Garth Turner began advising Canadians to stock up on beans, purchase guns, and prepare to dress in animal hides and survive on roadkill. The economy, not to mention the social order and the sky itself, was about to fall, they claimed. The world tilted on the brink of another Great Depression, this one far more destructive than the one of our grandparents' day.

Let's take a more rational approach, shall we?

Recessions and bear markets are neither rare nor unexpected. To a degree, they're actually beneficial. Think of them as forest fires that remove dead and diseased trees, encouraging vibrant new and healthy growth after things cool down and the sun and rain do their work. Instead of unhealthy trees, recessions wipe out incompetence and greed, and adjust debt loads and regulation to the proper levels for stable progress. As beneficial as forest fires and recessions may be, however, it is always wise to avoid being caught in the path of either one.

When Everybody Thinks the Same, Nobody Is Thinking at All

From 2002 to 2008, most economists preferred not to risk disagreeing with Alan Greenspan in case he happened to be proved correct, making them look incompetent. Greenspan, of course, was proved wrong and his reputation suffered dramatically. No one attacked the second-tier economists for being as mistaken as Greenspan because, hey, the Big Guy was the one who set the tone. When a handful of economists and commentators did actually speak up, few chose to listen. Martin Wolf, a highly regarded economist, wrote in his *Financial Times* column: "America's economy risks the mother of all meltdowns." This appeared in February 2008, long before the bottom fell out. Few people heeded his warning because Wolf was something of a maverick, and Alan Greenspan was, well, Alan Greenspan.

Wolf was a little late. Two years earlier, Nouriel Roubini, a professor of economics at New York University, made the same prediction and listed the 12 steps that would lead to the biggest economic setback since the 1930s. Among them, Roubini forecasted, would be a major collapse in stock prices, a drying-up of credit, and "a fire sale of assets at below fundamental prices."

Nobody was listening. Well, almost nobody.

In early 2008, I began receiving warnings from a B.C.–based investment analyst I know and trust. He noted that Citibank, the largest bank in the United States, was "essentially bankrupt." Warnings of inflation, worthless bonds, and a global retrenchment of trade began circulating among mavericks and independents who, in the opinion of establishment "experts," were one and the same. Almost everyone in the industry was aware of these warnings and understood both their logic and their implications.

So why didn't Suzanne Soucie's advisor heed them? Why did he insist on repeating the target price for bank shares set by his firm's analyst? For the same reason that the crew of an ocean liner doesn't change direction at the sight of an oncoming storm: because they are expected to be team players; because the guy on the bridge remains confident; and because large brokerages, like large ships, find it difficult to alter their charted course.

No one should expect any advisor or commentator to be correct in his or her assessment 100 percent of the time. Markets simply do not behave in a wholly predictable manner. Suzanne Soucie's advisor was correct in suggesting she move a portion of her RRSP equity assets into bank stocks, although he could be criticized for putting such a large portion of her RRSP into a single market sector.

But that's the point: When the next disaster doesn't announce its imminence, you have to assume it may be just around the corner. In all likelihood, the event will be another wave of rise-and-fall that is intrinsic to markets, and recovery may also be around the corner, although perhaps a block or two behind.

In your 20s, 30s, and into your 40s, down markets need not be critical as long as you remain employed. These are your earning years, after all. When you enter your 50s, however, your post-earning years become visible on the far horizon, and they insist on moving closer with every paycheque. That was Suzanne Soucie's point. She was grateful for the advice that enabled her to double her investment in less than seven years. But once it was gone, it appeared she would have to wait another seven years to recover her loss.

Here's an interesting thought: Had she invested the same amount of money in a guaranteed government-backed bond in 2001, one that would mature in 2015, she would have earned 5.5 percent interest annually, producing a 40 percent yield by 2008, untouched by the world's economic woes. In fact, her profits would be much higher than that because, by late 2008, interest rates for guaranteed bonds had tumbled to barely 2 percent annually; bond prices move counter to interest rates, and in early 2009, her bond would easily have doubled in price, providing her with a similar profit to her bank stocks—profit essentially free of risk.

Experience Is What You Get When You Were Expecting Something Else

Assessing the damage from the economic collapse of 2008–2009 to the RRSP accounts of Canadians is likely to continue for several years, but in the spring of 2009, one qualified source* estimated that the value of global capital losses may have exceeded US$50 trillion. Getting one's head around a trillion dollars is a problem for most people, no matter how large their Visa bills might be. So here's a measure: One trillion dollars is enough to inject $7000 into every household in the United States. Or, just to remind you how many zeros it takes to express this amount of money, read it this way: US$1,000,000,000,000. This will not make the losses your portfolio suffered any easier to take, but it does indicate the size of the problem. Even more impressive is the scope of the calamity.

Economic recessions since the Second World War have affected heavily industrialized nations most. In this most recent case, however, the impact is truly global, which makes it all the more frightening. China and India, two countries whose primarily agrarian and domestic-based economies made it easy to ride out economic storms in Europe and North America, have been knocked back as severely as the rest of the world. This is critical; the wider the impact, the longer it takes for everyone to recover because no sideline survivors exist to help the other players get back on their feet.

Here's another example of the scope, taken from both ends of the size spectrum:

In late 2008, Iceland came within a stiff breeze of being knocked into bankruptcy, thanks to excessive reliance on several banking ploys born of greed. The country remained on its feet with assistance from other nations, but it continues to face a national debt that will likely take generations to pay off.

---

*Global Financial Turmoil and Emerging Market Economies: Major Contagion and a Shocking Loss of Wealth, Asian Development Bank, March 2009.

Two points to make about Iceland: During the period 2004–2006, its economic performance shone like the polished star of unfettered capitalism. Assessed as one of the world's wealthiest countries on a per capita basis, it boasted an unemployment rate of less than 1 percent and an annual GDP growth rate of 5 percent. The country's population, by the way, is 320,000, which means it has fewer people than the city of London, Ontario.

So Iceland was a test-tube experiment on what happens when a country's overly aggressive government and banking leaders, if not its entire population, are blended with an explosive mixture of overextended loans and lack of fiscal restraint and regulation, and someone lights a match. If it all blows up, what's the real damage to the rest of the world? Not much.

But it's no longer a tempest in a test tube.

Expand the population to 142 million, call them Russians, perform the same experiment, and stand back. National bankruptcy for Russia remains a distinct possibility, with similar prospects for countries such as Argentina, Bolivia, Venezuela, and others. If these bankruptcies occur, we are no longer discussing a test-tube experiment but the demolition of much of the entire laboratory.

Such an event is unlikely for a number of reasons, but underestimating the number of rabid chickens intent on coming home to roost in future years is foolish in the extreme. By early 2009, the United States was acknowledging a debt of $18 trillion or, to put in all those zeros once again, $18,000,000,000,000,000. Serious stuff? Sure, but pocket change compared with the tsunami of debt rolling in from the far horizon. The U.S. federal government expects to spend $2 trillion annually for the next five years, adding $10 trillion to the bottom line. None of this includes the estimated $35 trillion ($35,000,000,000,000,000) in unfunded liabilities covering social security and Medicare that it will be required to pay over the same period.

This isn't merely a bill to be settled. It's an anchor to be dragged by the Good Ship America's economy through the next generation, and no one knows how it will affect the rest of the world during the next several years.

Government leaders and economists in the United States, many of them the same people who made reassuring noises about a strong economy back in mid-2008 before the debits hit the fan, are still trying to assess the full implications of this development and the best way of dealing with it. So far, they have not reached a consensus beyond spending money they don't have and, being politicians and economists, are not likely to. No matter how many assurances they hand out or policy changes they announce, no one can debate the axiom that too much debt is as lethal to a national economy, even one as large and vibrant as America's, as it is to your own household.

Until 2008, much of the debt in the United States could be identified as private debt. General Motors, AIG, Goldman Sachs, Citibank, and others carried enormous liabilities representing a burden primarily to themselves, their shareholders, and their creditors. Not good, but not universal either. The bailout practices of the American government, whatever their good intentions, have converted this private debt to public debt, to be carried on the backs of taxpayers.

They will need very strong backs for many years to come. Why? Because of a 50–50 split in income distribution among American households. According to income data from the U.S. Census 2006 Economic Survey, 50 percent of households in that country earn less than $50,000 annually. If we add the acknowledged U.S. debt level of $18,000,000,000,000 to the anticipated $2,000,000,000,000 debt to be recorded annually over the next five years at least, we can round off the public debt load at $28,000,000,000,000. As we've seen, each trillion is a $7000 debt load on every household in the United States, meaning *the average American household owes $196,000, or about four years of its total income.* Averages don't tell everything, of course. But in this case, they reveal the size of the burden.

It's old news that the enormous growth in the United States' gross domestic product (GDP) over the past quarter-century was financed by debt. Much of it, covered by credit cards and leveraged investments (where you put down 10 cents of your own money to make a $1 wager), was basically phoney borrowing, meaning, "I'll pay you back, but I don't know when or how."

What happens in Vegas may stay in Vegas, but what happens on Wall Street, Main Street, and everywhere business is conducted in the United States spills into Canada one way or another. When our neighbour's house is on fire, it's not enough to watch and feel complacent, because the wind is always blowing our way. As Canadians concerned about our own financial futures, our best plan is to fathom these developments and their attendant risks and construct our own protection against their most probable consequences. That's the fortress-investing mentality: Keep our hard-earned assets away from the barbarians on the other side of the moat, not to mention the world, while giving them enough room and sunlight to grow.

Maybe Not All Sunshine—But at Least a Silver Lining

So how are things in Canada? They could be worse.

As a trading nation, we are affected by economic problems virtually everywhere in the world, and as the closest neighbour and largest trading partner to the United States, we cannot escape shock waves originating south of the border. Yet, as integrated with the American economy as Canada might be, we escaped the worst of the economic debacle of 2008–2009, especially where our stock markets are concerned.

With Canada comfortably settled in its historical location midway between the United States and the United Kingdom, Canadian stock prices suffered measurably less damage than our southern neighbour's and noticeably less than the larger economies of Germany, Japan, and France. Moreover, our housing market, while shaken to its cellar doors, did not collapse in the manner of various regions of the United States because sub-prime mortgages, which awarded extravagant

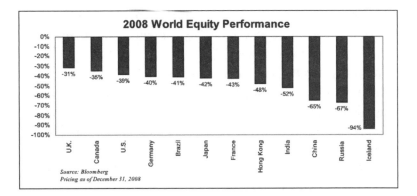

homes to buyers with less than extravagant incomes, were never a major factor here. Our large chartered banks, with their conservative lending policies, deserve credit as well; more than one international economic journal has rated our banking system the finest in the world—which doesn't quite balance the pain of their high fees, but never mind.

And since we're dependent on and similar to folks in the United States, at the risk of being labelled smug, let's step aside from questions of national debt and compare individual debt among their citizens and ours via the three critical measurements listed at the bottom of the page.

Faced with a primary trading partner holding a bill that is unlikely to be repaid for another generation or two, and a domestic economy

TYPE OF DEBT	U.S.A.	CANADA
Debt per Capita* (Canadian $)	$62,000	$35,000
Mortgage Debt—Share of Disposable Income	120%	80%
Consumer Debt—Share of Disposable Income	66%	52%

*Not including government (public) debt levels.
SOURCES: CIBC World Markets; *Report On Business Magazine*, February 2009.

that remains relatively healthy but limited in its scope (we're more of a commodities seller than a manufacturing nation), what can Canadians do to build and protect their investments, especially those directed toward post-employment years?

We'll cover this in following chapters. Meanwhile, here are a few ground rules to bear in mind:

1 Trade a portion of potential growth for a reasonable degree of certain security. The more growth you seek, the more risk you're taking. And the older you get, the less risk you can afford.

2 Unless you're comfortable taking your retirement savings to Vegas, don't try to outsmart the market. You will read about folks who look and sound very much like yourself scoring major returns for their RRSP and other investments by moving in and out of individual stocks like Bobby Orr stickhandling through a team of geriatric all-stars. This may make you feel like an underachiever. Do not let it. You will rarely hear of individuals who attempted the same manoeuvres and scored major losses. Among amateur or even semi-professional investors, their numbers are legion.

3 Avoid becoming desperate when markets turn downward. Desperate people do desperate things.

4 Inflation is coming. It may not be visible at the moment, but every move that governments around the world are making is inflationary. Be prepared.

5 Stay home for a while. In this case, "home" means Canada. Our markets are almost certain to be less volatile than those elsewhere in the world, especially emerging markets such as India, China, and most countries in South America. Volatility is the market player's friend. Market players are described in Rule 2 above.

Things Have Changed. Permanently.

The material-chasing, credit-driven growth witnessed over the past 25 years is out of fashion. Unless you measure your life's pleasures by the size of your yacht, this is not necessarily bad news.

Change is unsettling, even when we know it's inevitable and perhaps beneficial in the long run. This is especially true when we have little alternative except to adapt, whether we like it or not.

The changes produced by the economic crisis of 2008–2009 are hardly welcome if taken at face value. No one wants to see massive unemployment, deep government deficits, and the elimination of various perks and luxuries. Yet change brings opportunities as well, and opportunities are present on both sides of the line when it comes to retirement planning. They are there when we make the transition from a full-time wage or salary earner. And, more relevant to the topic at hand, they are there when we build our retirement nest egg.

The reality is acknowledged that we in North America (and much of Western Europe) have been living well beyond our means over the past quarter-century. Along with growing awareness and acceptance of the serious environmental impact our society has made, we can expect substantial shifts in our personal values and habits. It's not a stretch to suggest that personal energy once dedicated to creating wealth for the consumption of unneeded goods may now be invested in creating deep personal relationships with families and communities.

Before you dismiss this as Oprah dreaming in Disneyland, a similar shift in values occurred during the years of the Great Depression. We may already be witnessing such a change in various measurable ways. For example, in the years leading up to 2008, U.S. citizens had a negative savings rate, actually spending more than they were earning. Within a year, this shifted to a 4 percent savings rate, rising higher with each quarter. Limited credit card access, an emphasis on fuel-efficient transportation, and a growing awareness of the dangers of obesity, likely to match those of alcohol and tobacco, are certain to fuel the movement.

So where does this leave your retirement planning?

If, during your retirement years, you intended to maintain your effort to "keep up with the Joneses," forget it. Chances are the Joneses will be aiming to reduce their debt levels and search for fun closer to home instead of making their annual trek to Hawaii or the Caribbean.

Here's another factor you may not have linked to the changes occurring around us: We are living not only longer but more active lives. It's been pointed out that many Canadians will be spending more years in retirement than they spent at work. Many jobs have been made less stressful or boring, or otherwise more tolerable, and this has reduced the desperation in a lot of people just to get through their years of full-time employment. In the future, working beyond 60 or 65 on a reduced or part-time basis may become as attractive as retirement—and would certainly be more profitable.

The Startling Notion of "First Retirement"

Instead of bursting our chains and thumbing our nose at the boss in a "full-stop" retirement, we may actually retire in two stages.

"First Retirement" could include reducing the number of working hours with our current employer, negotiating a new relationship as a consultant, or providing other contractual services built on the skills and experience we have acquired over the years. This idea is very appealing to many employers who understand that a productive employee walking out the door, either through layoff or retirement, represents a lost asset. If this same source of productivity is available on a reduced cost or "as needed" basis, such a proposition becomes economically attractive. You may also choose to leave your current workplace entirely but find employment in another position and another industry or service, perhaps on a part-time basis.

These First Retirement years can be pleasant and rewarding, leaving you more time for activities you enjoy, such as golf or volunteer work, and reducing pressure on your retirement income. With an outside income, some interesting financial alternatives become available. If you have converted your RRSP to a RRIF, currently compulsory at the end of the year you turn 71 years of age, you are locked into a formula requiring you to make minimum annual withdrawals. Your First Retirement plan may generate enough income that you don't need all the cash from your RRIF and Canada/Quebec Pension Plan (C/QPP) benefits, especially if your mortgage is paid up and your children are living on their own. You could deposit up to $5000 of your RRIF income each year into a tax-free savings account (TFSA) for future growth free of income tax, supplementing your savings for future years. Eventually, you would move into a Second Retirement, when your entire income is provided by your savings and investments, a move dictated perhaps by health concerns and reduced energy.

These are possibilities, not certainties. In any event, both alternatives require the financial security provided by a substantial asset base to replace your lost income from full employment, even with those reduced household expenses. Unless, of course, you'll enjoy spending your retirement years in a rocking chair, nibbling baloney sandwiches. That's not me, and it shouldn't be you or anyone perceptive enough to have foreseen their retirement needs during their working years and been prudent enough to have done something about it.

Those of us who faithfully contributed to an RRSP or defined-contribution pension over our working years should, at 50-plus years of age, begin paying as much attention to the preservation of capital as to the growth of our retirement assets.

That's the basis of this book, and it has never been more important.

2

THERE'S NEVER ENOUGH LEFT
OVER FOR THE LITTLE GUY

Sarah Herjavec* feels like a victim, and it both angers and saddens her. During her 35 years with Northern Telecom/Nortel, she fulfilled all her obligations as a management employee, taking training courses, working weekends without extra pay, and eventually rising to the level of executive assistant to the senior vice-presidents of the firm. She also invested a substantial amount of her RRSP in Nortel stock with the encouragement of her boss.

On January 11, 2009, just three days before Nortel filed for bankruptcy, she lost her job. She was 55 years old and entitled to a monthly pension of about $2500, which would help pay her mortgage and support her teenaged son in high school. But two years earlier, the Nortel pension plan was estimated to be under-funded by almost $2 billion; by the time the company sought bankruptcy protection, the pension shortfall had reached an estimated $2.8 billion.

"I don't know if I'm going to ever receive a pension," Herjavec says, "or how much." The losses suffered by the decline of Nortel stock, from $120 per share to the price of a Tim Hortons coffee within a few months, crushed her RRSP as well as her spirit.

---

*A pseudonym.

Former Nortel CEO John Roth, whom many blame for the fall of Nortel from a globally admired electronic icon to a near-empty shell, is not crushed—not economically at least. Roth was paid about $160 million from 1999 to 2001 when he was at the helm of the sinking ship and pocketed an additional $135 million in stock options—conveniently sold just before the share price shrank to penny-stock status.

In July 2009, several months after Nortel filed for bankruptcy protection, employees on long-term disability discovered that, contrary to the information they reportedly received from company management over the years, their disability benefits were not insured by Sun Life Assurance but were funded by a division of Nortel itself, in an obviously flawed attempt to save money.* The news added another devastating layer to the tragedy, because Nortel's collapse would prevent it from continuing to pay disability benefits.

It's not known if the company's difficulties in meeting its pension and other employee benefits obligations will affect Roth's cash flow. Based on 30-plus years of service (about the same number of years Sarah Herjavec put in with the company) and his hefty salary just before he stepped down, Roth's pension was speculated in media reports to be "exceptionally generous"—meaning somewhere in the mid-six-figures each year.

If it's any comfort to Sarah Herjavec and thousands of other Canadians who find themselves in similar straits, they are definitely not alone. Even those Canadians who remain employed fear their financial future has been clouded by the events of 2008–2009.

In 2007, Canadians held almost $2 trillion in RRSPs and employee pension plans, a comfortable nest egg. By early 2009, the value of

---

*Karen Mazurkewich, "Nortel's Disabled Benefits May Go," *Financial Post*, July 8, 2009.

these same accounts had fallen by $400 billion or more, with the biggest losses suffered by people nearest to their retirement date.*

The urgent need to fix this problem cannot be ignored. Thanks to the baby boom and the positive impact of our health-care system, more older Canadians are around and they're living longer. In 2005, about 13 percent of Canadians were age 65 or older; by 2031, more than one out of every four Canadians will be in that category. As many as one out of four Canadians under 65 could be unemployed due to youth, illness, or other reasons, leaving just two Canadians earning enough income and paying enough taxes to support almost all the cost of CPP, OAS, health-care expenditures, and other drains on government budgets.

The major recession that began in mid-2007 drove some people to suggest the world was facing another Great Depression, a period that began with financiers allegedly throwing themselves out of skyscraper windows (though in reality, only one individual solved his personal fiscal crisis in this manner) and ended with Nazi Germany invading Poland.

Beyond their global scope, the two economic crises had almost nothing else in common. The Depression was triggered by unrealistic stock prices creating a bubble that no one believed would burst; the recession of 2007–2009 was caused by outrageous manipulation of credit by unregulated traders and brokerages. The reactions by those in power are even more contrasting. Depression-era governments chose a do-nothing policy with the exception of the United States, where the Smoot-Hawley Tariff Act effectively stifled international trade and exacerbated the situation. Current governments are playing an active role—some claim it's overactive—to assist key sectors in their economies. And the social safety net we depend upon today was non-existent in the 1930s.

Still, past experience at least provides the opportunity to review the four major economic recessions to affect Canada during the past

---

*Sandro Contenta, "When Retirement Savings Tank," *Toronto Star*, March 15, 2009.

century. It's enlightening to note that the first two incidents ended in a world war, one risk we may be able to discount. Admittedly, the wars stimulated economies everywhere, but surely we can implement a more humane and less destructive solution.

1904–1914. The first of two major stock market collapses ended a 10-year period of strong economic growth. A major meltdown of stock prices in 1907 knocked the New York Stock Exchange almost out of existence—a fate that a dozen major banks and trust companies could not avoid when Americans began pulling money out of their accounts. Canadian markets were seriously affected and the country's GDP fell three years in a row.

1929–1939. The Roaring Twenties ended with the burst of the stock market bubble. In Canada, unemployment hit 27 percent and GDP dropped 43 percent thanks to the impact of the Smoot-Hawley Tariff Act, which cut global trade by 65 percent.

The early 1980s. Energy prices soared and Canadian GDP fell 7 percent in less than 18 months. The resulting inflation rate rose to double digits, and prime lending rates moved from about 8 percent in 1970 to a crippling 19 percent in 1981.

The early 1990s. Canada caught a milder case of the same disease it had suffered 10 years earlier. Interest rates reached 14 percent, the unemployment level surpassed 10 percent, and GDP fell more than 2 percent in one year.

In 2009. Unemployment exceeded 7 percent—not good but not nearly as debilitating as previous occasions—and interest rates were a penny's thickness above zero, an unprecedented event. Perhaps the most serious indicator: GDP fell almost 3.5 percent in the last quarter of 2008 and export levels maintained a two-year decline.

Getting Back on Track

If, like most Canadians, you suffered a loss of 40 percent or more in the value of equities within your RRSP, RRIF, TFSA, or unregistered portfolio, the challenge of recovering these losses and restoring your anticipated growth may be more complex than you expect. The reason? It takes a longer period of growth to correct the same amount of loss.

A simple 40 percent gain cannot offset a loss of the same measure. Losing 40 percent of $1000 leaves $600. Earning a 40 percent gain on the $600 residue generates only $240, increasing the value of your investment to a mere $840. You'll actually need more than 66 percent in growth before you climb back to $1000. Whenever this occurs, you'll still be in a loss position because you missed out on anticipated growth during the recovery years. If you had planned on a reasonable 5 percent annual growth in your portfolio and it takes seven years from the date your assets are valued at $1000 through their slide to $600 and back to the original $1000 again, you've missed 35 percent in anticipated growth.

As long as you're aiming for 5 percent annual real growth in your assets, you will never catch up to where you might have been before the substantial loss. This may inspire you, especially if your retirement is within sight, to seek substantially more growth as a means of reaching the level you expect to attain before things fall apart. Actually, the inspiration may originate with greedy financial advisors who anticipate building more increases in their assets than in yours. (For details on the dangers of this development, see Chapter 6: Paying for "Expert" Advice that Profits the Other Guy.)

The challenge of overcoming major losses for RRSP owners post-2009 is twofold. First challenge: Get investments back to the same value as they had before the TSX began its long slide from 15,000 in June 2007 to barely half that by March 2009. Second challenge: Get back on track to achieve the targeted goal ASAP. These tasks are more challenging than many RRSP/RRIF investors may expect.

Here are four typical scenarios for investors seeking to hit both targets. Note that they are realistic, based on annual growth rates over the past 20 years, which are the targeted annual gains they might expect.

1 **Jane.** 60 years of age, employed part-time, 55% of portfolio in short-term government bonds and three-year GICs; 45% in mixed equities.

Value of RRSP at March 2007:	$200,000
Value of RRSP at July 2009:	$145,000
Target annual growth rate:	7%
Date to get back on track (for retirement):	December 2014
Original target RRSP value (at retirement):	$338,000
Average annual return needed to reach target:	15.8%

2 **Jack.** 68 years of age, self-employed, 50% of portfolio in bonds, 50% in three equity-based mutual funds.

Value of RRSP at March 2007:	$400,000
Value of RRSP at July 2009:	$305,000
Target annual growth rate:	7%
Date to get back on track (for retirement):	December 2011
Original target RRSP value (at retirement):	$550,000
Average annual return needed to reach target:	24.0%

3 **Jasmine.** 50 years of age, widowed, 50% of portfolio in cash, 50% in one equity-based mutual fund.

Value of RRSP at March 2007:	$30,000
Value of RRSP at July 2009:	$21,000
Target annual growth rate:	8%

Date to get back on truck (for retirement):	March 2010
Target RRSP value:	$40,800
Average annual return needed to reach target:	94.3%

4 **Jay.** 35 years of age, employed, 80% of portfolio in equities, 20% in cash.

Value of RRSP at March 2007:	$18,000
Value of RRSP at July 2009:	$10,800
Target annual growth rate:	7%
Date to get back on track:	March 2030
Target RRSP value (at retirement):	$120,000
Average annual return to needed reach target:	12.75%

These calculations do not include contributions that each RRSP owner may make between July 2009 and their target date.

It's not unusual for markets to post double-digit yields when economies turn around, so 14 to 20 percent gains for a year or two are not impossible. In fact, they may be anticipated in the wake of the 2008–2009 recession because recessions tend to make companies more efficient. Layoffs that occur in bad economic times enable corporations to run lean with smaller staffs working at greater efficiencies, and bad debts often are washed off the books in one all-encompassing bath under tough conditions. As a result, when customers return and orders resume their previous volume, profits often expand dramatically with a corresponding increase in share price. Still, it pays to be conservative, and since the 7 to 8 percent gains mark the realistic levels anticipated prior to the 2008–2009 crash, they have been used here.

Jane's back-on-track target appears reasonable, assuming she catches a ride on a rapidly rising market, although five and a half years of 15-plus percent average annual returns is too much to expect. Jack's target recovery is also unlikely. He needs only two and a half years of 24 percent gains. This has been known to happen, but people have also been known to discover oil in their backyards.

Jasmine's hope of reaching her goal is simply unrealistic, and Jay will need to average 12.75 percent annually over 20 years, also unlikely. He can expect to be sideswiped by inflation along the way too.

When You Can't Change the Facts, Change the Goal

Two alternatives present themselves. One is to find a way of generating the high returns needed to achieve the original targeted portfolio size—more about this later. The other is to move the retirement target date back, lowering the required level of growth and extending the investment period. Here's how the strategy works with each of our four examples; the extra years are in addition to those that the investor had planned before the market fell, reducing the annual yield needed:

			EXTRA YEARS NEEDED		
NAME	TARGET	YIELD	2	4	8
Jane	$338,000	15.8%	13.5%	11.2%	10.6%
Jack	$550,000	24.0%	16.6%	13.6%	11.1%
Jasmine	$40,800	94.3%	31.4%	21.5%	15.3%
Jay	$120,000	12.75%	11.6%	10.5%	9.0%

As dismal as these figures appear, they deliver an important lesson about not attempting to recover all of your retirement investment losses within a short period of time. Nor should you abandon forever the idea of seeking growth in your portfolio through stock market investments. The fact remains that equity markets deliver the best opportunities to increase your asset base, leading to a much more rewarding—and relaxing—retirement.

Make no mistake: The economic crisis of 2008–2009 will change many aspects of life around the globe forever. Its impact will be felt not just economically but politically and socially as well. A very long time will pass before financial and investment markets around the world will be permitted once again to operate in the same Wild West style that they carried on from 1980 to 2008. Back in the heyday of the Reagan–Thatcher years, regulation was viewed as a government-related disease, an illness that crippled profit-seeking corporations and strengthened power-hungry governments. Maybe so. But the medicine of deregulation has proved at least as crippling as the disease of excessive government oversight.

The only available cure for the globe's economic ailment has been provided by national governments, the group that laissez-faire political conservatives once vilified as scoundrels intent on shrinking the fruits of capitalism. By 2009, the largest banks, manufacturing centres, and insurance providers in the United States had all effectively been nationalized in an action that, just a few years earlier, would have sent the country's right-wing factions to the barricades.

The impact is certain to be felt socially as well. Business people in the United States and elsewhere are trumpeting the growth prospects of firms engaged in developing and marketing efficient and alternative-source energy systems. Meanwhile, older Canadians, Americans, and Europeans are reassessing the concept of "retirement," a period once labelled the Golden Years and best illustrated by a woman doing needlework at a cottage window while her slouch-hatted husband wanders down the lane, fishing pole over his shoulder and dog tagging along behind.

Retirement in the next decade of the 21st century will resemble that image the way a ping-pong ball resembles a bowling ball. Instead of abandoning the active world, future retirees will either extend their employment years out of choice, because they enjoy their work, or out of necessity, because they cannot afford to lose the income. Age, decay, and disease eventually claim all of us, but many will remain active and alert far longer than our parents and grandparents did, leaving many more options beyond needlework and fishing.

All of this must be assessed against the reality of potentially limited retirement income based on vanishing defined-benefit pensions in the private sector, and reduced (for the immediate future at least) prospects of substantial growth from RRSP and TFSA investments.

How do we deal with this? By taking four steps, each reflecting guidelines to be discussed in later chapters. Remember: *You cannot maximize the growth in your RRSP, RRIF, or TFSA without adding an equivalent degree of risk. And you must not exceed a definable and acceptable level of risk in the last few years prior to winding down your RRSP.* The four steps:

1 **Keep making RRSP and TFSA contributions; if possible, increase your contributions.** It may be difficult to think of saving for the future when the stock market is depressed, but it's a clever move. If you drove past a gas station advertising a price per litre that was 50 percent lower than elsewhere, wouldn't you pull over and fill your tank at the bargain rate? The key here is to invest your contributions in quality stocks or indexed mutual funds that mirror the stock market (details in Chapter 5). Emerging from the 2008–2009 recession, most stocks remain underpriced. Buy them when low and fix a future price to sell and take profits. One more time: Nobody ever went broke taking profits.

2 **Learn the principle and techniques of asset allocation.** Many successful investors claim ideally allocating the correct proportion of your portfolio in stocks (including equity-based mutual funds), bonds and GICs (referred to as debt instruments), and cash (including money market funds) is the key to success at maximizing earnings. Asset allocation involves securing a rock-solid foundation for your portfolio with debt instruments and cash, and obtaining growth through equity investments. The relative proportion of each, determined by your age and risk tolerance, requires adjustment from time to time. Details on asset allocation are covered in following chapters.

3 **Diversification still works—usually.** The old adage about not putting all your eggs in one basket didn't seem all that perceptive throughout 2008–2009 when every basket on stock exchanges around the world fell, creating basket-sized omelettes. Nothing works when there are no winners. Diversification does work, however, during a generally climbing market. If you choose individual stocks, select the best of various core industries. In Canada, this is limited to banks and financial firms, resources, and limited manufacturing and technology. If possible, vary the company size and the markets they serve, with small-cap (under $500 million in capitalization) as well as larger firms, and domestic as well as international companies. With mutual funds, select funds based on different broadly based markets and sectors, keeping an eye on costs charged to you by the fund.

4 **Don't give up on the market.** The stock market is not an oak tree, steadily reaching for the sky above a solid base; it's an endless roller coaster that keeps trying to carry riders higher and higher—and often succeeds—before dropping to regain new momentum. Trees will keep growing toward the sun, encouraged by periodic

watering, feeding, and pruning. Very nice. But unless you invest in a highly successful lumber company, trees won't maximize your retirement fund.

For all its trapdoors, potholes, banana skins, and cul-de-sacs, the stock market remains your best investment option, risks and all. In many ways, it's like the world outside your bedroom window. You can huddle under the bed and feel safe, or you can step outside and feel alive, maybe even prosperous. Just remember how the world works, and act accordingly.

Is It Different This Time?

In assessing human behaviour during periods of change and upheaval, psychologists refer to *anchored expectations*, meaning we expect the future to be very much like the past. People who grew up during the Great Depression of the 1930s feared debt and the loss of their jobs, and assumed that the risk of a repeat performance was imminent or at least possible. Those of us who matured and went to work in the 1950s, 1960s, and 1970s assumed there would always be a way to earn enough money to survive and prosper.

This latter point of view was trumpeted with great glee by mutual fund marketers, financial advisors, and even people like Warren Buffett. "Buy and hold," Buffett preached, and he was generally correct, backed by statistics demonstrating it was almost impossible to lose money on quality stocks held over a 10-year period. Give an equity portfolio enough time, and yourself enough patience, and you can't lose, said pundits and mutual fund hucksters. Maybe true, but it is also difficult to drown in a river only 20 centimetres deep unless, of course, that's merely the average depth.

The economic crisis of 2008–2009 changed everyone's thinking, even Buffett's. From September 2008 to March 2009, the price of one Class A share in Buffett's Berkshire Hathaway Inc., perhaps the most highly regarded investment fund in the business, dropped from \$147,000 to \$70,050, a teeth-chattering collapse of more than 50 percent.

So here comes the lesson: Time in the market is no guarantee of profit, and the closer you approach the day your RRSP investment morphs from a piggy bank to a cash machine, the more critical this realization becomes.

We can become lost in statistics while swinging from deep despair about losses to high elation over the prospect of triple-digit annual growth. We can also ignore economic statistics and crawl under the bed, refusing to emerge until something akin to sanity and stability returns.

Hiding under the bed achieves nothing except covering yourself in dust bunnies. The real world is noisy, risky, sometimes dangerous, and often rewarding. Let's get out in it.

3

THE VERY BIG LIE THE
INVESTMENT INDUSTRY TELLS YOU
ABOUT RISK

The death of Jack Tindale's* wife after almost 50 years of marriage affected the 74-year-old retired executive in more ways than he expected. Following the advice of his children, he continued to maintain a townhouse in Ottawa and a condominium in Florida, where Tindale and his wife had spent many winters. Their friends in Florida, Tindale and his children knew, would provide the support he needed to counterbalance the nostalgia and depression he felt over the absence of his wife.

In fact, the only substantial change Tindale made was to alter the way he managed his RRIF. He and his wife had made their own investment decisions, using a discount broker, and he had valued his wife's suggestions and opinions. Without her participation he lacked the will and confidence to continue making these decisions, and transferred his RRIF account, which now included assets in his wife's RRIF, to an independent investment broker.

"I want a balanced portfolio," he instructed the advisor before leaving for Florida in January, "with about 70 percent in bonds or some other income-producing investment and the balance in

---

*A pseudonym. Based on "Investors Must Watch Advisors," by Ellen Roseman in the *Toronto Star*, March 22, 2009.

blue-chip stocks." The advisor agreed, asked Tindale to sign a few documents, and wished him a happy winter in the sun.

When Tindale returned home in April and opened his statements from the investment dealer, he was appalled to discover that 80 percent of his portfolio had been transferred into deferred sales charge (DSC) mutual funds that had already lost more than 10 percent of their book value. Calling the broker, he demanded the mutual funds be disposed of and the money invested according to his wishes. "If you do that," the advisor informed him, "you will be docked about $15,000 in sales charges." Tindale was appalled. He hadn't chosen the funds; the advisor did. Why should he pay a penalty for the advisor's bad decision? He insisted that the investment company absorb the fees; the company refused, claiming that Tindale had no cause for complaint because the advisor had made a decision according to Tindale's requirements.

Furious, Tindale contacted the Investment Industry Regulatory Organization of Canada (IIROC), created from the consolidation of the Investment Dealers Association of Canada (IDA) and Market Regulation Services Inc. IIROC's mandate, according to the organization's documents, is to "set and enforce high quality regulatory and investment industry standards, protect investors and strengthen market integrity while maintaining efficient and competitive capital markets." Its vision (how did corporations function in the days before each had to have a vision?) is "(to) be known for our integrity, our transparency and our fair and balanced solutions. We aim for excellence and regulatory best practices. Our actions are driven by sound, intelligent deliberation and consultation."

IIROC rejected Tindale's complaint outright. "You authorized every trade processed in your account," an IIROC enforcement officer lectured him, "including the purchase of mutual funds," referring to the documents Tindale signed before leaving for Florida. With no evidence of a regulatory breach the case was closed, leaving Tindale with the choice of watching his ill-performing mutual funds continue to decline faster than the stock market or paying $15,000 to bail them out in the hope of locating more suitable investments.

IIROC appeared to have based its decision exclusively upon Tindale's granting his advisor the power to select and purchase investments according to Tindale's needs and situation. IIROC, like its predecessor the IDA, did not look beyond the granting of this authority to judge the suitability of investments chosen for Tindale's portfolio. Tindale and millions of Canadians like him agree to such an arrangement because they perceive that advisors will base their decisions according to what is best for the client. They do not. Not all of them.

Commission-paid advisors, like the one assigned to Jack Tindale's account, earn very little money from dealing in bonds, GICs, exchange traded funds (ETFs)* and similar investments, compared with the earnings they generate from DSC mutual funds with large management expense ratios (MERs), similar to those placed by the advisor in Tindale's portfolio.

IIROC may have changed its name, its mandate, and its vision but has not changed its policy of essentially ignoring the suitability of investment decisions and actions taken by advisors. Once a client signs an agreement authorizing an advisor to make trades, most of the ensuing decisions are considered sacrosanct by IIROC.

It's an interesting position. Imagine that a surgeon, treating you for a gastro-intestinal problem caused by your gall bladder, asks you to sign a release form authorizing a procedure to be carried out according to the surgeon's perception of your needs. You agree and discover, after awakening from the anaesthesia, that the surgeon chose to remove

---

*For a detailed discussion of ETFs, see Chapter 5: Crisis-Resistant Investments: How Much Assistance Do You Need to Acquire Them?

your healthy appendix instead. Not only has your problem not been solved; you later discover that the surgeon earns more from an appendectomy than a gall bladder procedure. Can you imagine the surgeon's action being successfully defended based upon your signature on a release form, and subsequently supported by a medical review board that claimed the decision had been made in your interest with your prior approval in principle and could not be criticized?

Investment industry defenders may claim that their decisions are hardly life-or-death issues, but this is true only to a point if you are age 60-plus and discover your RRSP portfolio has been devastated by inappropriate investments and heavy fees. Claims that IIROC may make about representing investor interests are, to say the least, subject to serious doubt. In a few instances, the organization has agreed that advisors of member organizations acted in defiance of guidelines, and actually recovered commissions earned by these renegades through their corrupt actions. When clients whose ravaged accounts were the source of funds from these unauthorized actions asked for their money back, they were told it had been transferred to the coffers of the IDA/IIROC to finance the organization's activities and would not be returned.* Another analogy: Someone steals cash from your home, is caught and convicted, and the money is recovered. You ask the courts for your money. You are told, "Sorry, we need it to redecorate the courthouse." That's how IIROC works.

This policy is contributing to a reassessment of millions of Canadians regarding the wisdom of relying upon licensed advisors and full-service investment houses. Do-it-yourself investors make errors in their investment decisions, most of which can be avoided by following basic guidelines. But substantial savings in sales commissions and fees may offset to at least some degree any losses suffered due to inappropriate decisions.

---

*For details on these and other actions by the IDA/IIROC and other investment industry organizations that appear to favour advisors over clients, please see my book *The Naked Investor: Why Almost Everybody But You Gets Rich on your RRSP.*

If you cannot rely upon licensed professionals to always act in your best interests rather than according to the sales commissions they generate for themselves—and cannot expect either a sympathetic response or any effort to replace losses experienced through the actions of others—how much worse can things become by acting as your own investment counsellor?

Beware the Investment Wisdom of Kitchen Help

Some profitable investment decisions are based on wisdom and experience. Others are the result of luck and circumstance. And a few are the product of realistic expectations. Like this one:

Back in the mid-1990s, I purchased a few hundred shares of Nortel Networks within my RRSP. I knew a fair bit about the firm, foresaw the internet-based industry expanding at a rapid clip, and figured the company was well managed by prudent Canadians.

I was proven correct when the shares more than doubled over the next three or four years, topping $100 per share in early 2000. That January, during an annual review of my portfolio with my financial advisor, I instructed him to sell the shares.

He was incredulous. "Our analysts are setting a target price of $130 a share, maybe higher," he said. "You could be missing out on some major gains."

I agreed that I might, but I didn't care. Two things were influencing me.

First, I had more than doubled my investment in a relatively short time. I don't believe I am less greedy than the average Canadian, but it seemed to me that I had earned as much or more than might be expected. Besides, the higher the climb, the greater the risk of the price tumbling. Stocks always swing past their true value, which triggers a fall—known in the industry as a "correction," as though an error had been made. My advisor believed the error was still sometime in the future. I was convinced, however, that the chance I might make more profit from the stock was speculation; the fact that I had already more than doubled my money was reality. I chose reality. If the analysts at my financial advisor's firm were proved correct and I missed out on another $20 or $30 gain per share by year's end, I wouldn't regret it. I was guided by growth more than greed.

My other reason for selling was essentially instinctive but equally valid.

A week or so earlier, my wife and I were dining in a mid-priced restaurant not far from Bay Street in Toronto. Our table was not in a prestigious location; in fact it was adjacent to the busboys' station, where empty plates and utensils were parked before being carried off to the dishwasher.

Midway through our meal, a waiter and busboy struck up a conversation near the stacked china littered with scraps of steak and vegetables. I wasn't eavesdropping; it was impossible not to pick up their words.

"So," the waiter said, "did you get those Nortel shares I told you about?"

"I got five," the busboy said. "All I could afford at a hundred bucks apiece."

"Shoulda got more," the waiter lectured. "Way I hear it, they'll be up to a hundred and fifty by summer."

"You buying more?" the busboy said, hefting a tray piled high with dining detritus.

"Much as I can," the waiter replied, turning on his heel and heading back toward the centre of the restaurant where Bay Street traders, analysts, and brokers were seated.

I have enormous respect for people engaged in the hospitality industry. Their working conditions include long hours, variable compensation, and frequent encounters with boorish customers. I also assume that serving staff and busboys are as intelligent and perceptive as average Canadians. But when the waiter and busboy began exchanging investment advice regarding a company that had scored dramatic increases in its value and represented almost 30 percent of the entire capitalization of the Toronto Stock Exchange, I feared the bandwagon was in danger of losing its wheels. By the time an insight into Nortel's future value travelled from corporate boardrooms to waiters and busboys, the value of any investment opinion was already being discounted by the market.

I trust this will not set off a flurry of cards and letters charging me with insulting restaurant and kitchen staff as investment-illiterate dunces. It's not true. I hasten to add that some of the most nonsensical investment ideas I've ever heard emanated from the fallow minds of retired teachers, aggressive business executives, and head-scratching academics. It wasn't the wait staff's occupation that tripped a red light in my mind. It was the gap between those who honestly know what's going on and those who *think* they know. My financial advisor had been saying the same thing as the waiter and busboy, and I figure he's right maybe 55 percent of the time. The restaurant staff? Gotta be less than that. Much less. It was my cue to get out, and I did.

Within a month, the price of Nortel stock began to drop, taking tens of thousands of jobs with it and the retirement dreams of at least as many investors. I experienced no *schadenfreude* watching the long painful slide of the shares to penny-stock status, nor any pride in my decision. I just recalled the wisdom of a loving aunt who cared for me as a young child and deflected my craving for a new toy or new item of clothing by saying, "First, be satisfied with what you have." Any time you have been fortunate or clever enough to double your money within two or three years, be satisfied with your success and move on.

This is one place where buy and hold no longer applies. In its place, think, "Buy and, when the price doubles, sell half."

The Small Lie within a Larger Truth

My book *Free Rider: How a Bay Street Whiz Kid Stole and Spent $20 Million* opened my eyes to some realities of the investment industry I had not been aware of earlier. One was the gap between how much the industry understands about investing and how little the vast majority of investors know.

The investment industry justifies its fees and commissions by bridging this gap. That's a reasonable basis for operating a business. I have no idea how the automatic transmission of my car works, let alone how to dismantle and repair it. If something goes wrong with the transmission's innards after the warranty expires, I pay to have it repaired. Part of that cost will reflect the transmission mechanic's training, expertise, and experience. And if the mechanic tells me why the problem occurred and how to prevent it from happening again, I'll listen closely and take the advice seriously.

The differences between an automobile transmission and your RRSP portfolio are obvious and extensive. The expectation of receiving value for your money, however, should remain comparable. Sad to say, it's often not.

Should you religiously follow the guidance of your advisor and discover that, instead of providing clear direction about investing conservatively and practising caution, the advisor's actions have produced losses dramatically in excess of the overall market, any concerns expressed by you will receive the response "all investment decisions involve risk." If your losses are sufficiently catastrophic for you to seek legal action, through all the stages of consideration, arbitration, and adjudication the mantra will be rephrased as: *When you choose to invest, you choose to accept risk.*

True. But hardly valid.

Risk is everywhere. Hiding your money in your mattress involves risk. Sliding all your RRSP contributions into a bank account risks lowering its buying power due to inflation. *Risk and reward are conjoined twins; the more you expect of one, the more you accept of the other.*

Nobody gives away something for nothing. Nobody will give you more growth for your investment without getting something in return, and the "something" is increased risk. That's a universal truth. But the fact that you must accept the loss of risk in your RRSP balance that mirrors the loss in a stock market is not true. It is an outright lie.

After spending more than a decade researching complaints of advisor incompetence, malfeasance, and outright manipulation of client assets for their own gain, I have found that advisors and their firms use the "investment involves risk" defence with remarkable success. It's more than a maxim: It's a Get out of Jail Free card that accompanies every advisor's licence.

Here's a truth rarely revealed: Risk can be measured to a remarkably accurate degree and, once accounted for, it can be balanced to neutralize or diminish the impact of disaster. You cannot completely avoid risk, but you can reduce it by controlling the extreme and unexpected rise and fall of stock market prices.

At Last—A Chance to Use Your High School Algebra

Your idea of measuring investment risk may be to read the newspapers, listen to commentators on TV news channels, absorb mutual fund promotional material, and talk to your friends. All well and good. But this is like hoping to become a fashion model by subscribing to *Vogue*. You may be immersed in the culture, but you're removed from the reality. When dealing with risk and volatility, you need more practical methods, although they needn't be as technical as those used by heavy-duty investment managers who probe, dissect, and evaluate risk.

Risk management is a highly skilled and very important profession, practised by PhDs and folks of lesser qualifications employing calculations as complex and precise as anything NASA uses. People you have never heard of, and likely will never meet, spend each working day performing calculations such as:

$$Rit - Rft = ai + bi (Rmt - Rft) + si\ SMBt + hi\ HMLt + eit$$

It's not a formula for growing hair. It's the basic calculation for the Fama-French Three-Factor Model, used to compare an investment portfolio with the market as a whole, weighing risk against return. For everyone who did well in high school algebra and wants to show off their retained facility, here are the components of the quotation. The rest of us will take a break to file our nails:

> *Rit* is the return to portfolio *i* for month *t*.
> *Rft* is the T-bill return for month *t*.
> *Rmt* is the return to the CRSP value-weighted index for month *t*.
> *SMBt* is the realization on a capitalization-based factor portfolio that buys small-cap stocks and sells large-cap stocks.
> Similarly, *HMLt* is the realization on a factor portfolio that buys high-BtM stocks and sells low-BtM stocks.
> The *si* and *hi* coefficients measure the sensitivity of the portfolio's return to the small-minus-big and high-minus-low factors, respectively. Portfolios of value stocks will have a high value for *h*, while growth portfolios will have a negative *h*. Large-cap portfolios will load negatively on *SMB* (*si* will be negative), and small-cap portfolios will have a positive value for *s*.

I'm hardly suggesting that you or your advisor (if you have one) evaluate your portfolio's risk and performance by using this formula. It's here to demonstrate that *investment risk can be measured precisely and, once measured, steps can be taken to avoid disaster.* This tool, and the knowledge it provides, are set down here to belie the caveat that investors must accept risk and, having accepted it, are required to forgive their advisors for any devastating consequences of the advisor's guidance.

The concept of measuring risk is hardly restricted to the investment industry. Engineers building a bridge, surgeons planning a procedure, and pilots filing a flight plan all weigh risk and make decisions accordingly. The method of measuring risk is different in each case, to be sure. For the bridge engineer, the primary risk may be a factor of time; if the bridge is expected to perform safely for 25 years, the risk can be mitigated by various design elements. For the surgeon, the main risk could be personal: Does that surgeon have sufficient training, experience, and facilities to perform the procedure safely? For the pilot, it may be a go or no-go decision: Is the weather forecast favourable? Does the aircraft have the range to reach the destination?

Whether it's keeping you and your car from tumbling into a valley, flying you to Europe, or providing as much protection as possible for your retirement savings, all professionals employ the same basic five-step guide to risk management:

1 Identify the risk: What can go wrong and when? Where will it happen?

2 Quantify the risk: How serious will it be? How widespread? How much will it cost to avoid or reduce it?

3 Measure the probability of each risk occurring: Is the likelihood high or low?

4 Evaluate the impact: How much damage will it cause?

5 Create plans to reduce the risk and/or the amount of damage: What can be saved, and how?

Finding the most effective way of maximizing the growth of your RRSP and minimizing the risk that it will be in the tank before you're in the money involves using as many ways of reducing the risk factor as possible.

And here's the kicker: Some of them start with *you.*

It's Not Just Mechanical—It's Also Personal

Few of us will build a sturdy bridge, perform life-saving surgery, or guide an aircraft through stormy weather. We rely on others better equipped in every way to perform these jobs for us. We cannot expect to rely to the same degree on those who are guiding us in our investment decisions.

To be sure, there are no absolutes in investment management. Saving 90 percent of your RRSP assets in a falling market is acceptable; safely flying passengers 90 percent of the way across the Atlantic is not. But your involvement in measuring and diminishing the risk to your portfolio can be far more active than your role as an airline passenger would be.

One way you can achieve this is by avoiding hazards that occur when greed overtakes wisdom. It's not so much that the greed level among Canadians is high; it's because basic understanding of investment fundamentals is so low. Here's a good example:

Beginning in the 1990s, many financial advisors in Canada were bombarded by requests from clients about mutual funds. Usually they weren't requests at all but demands: Put me into hedge funds!

Hedge funds are a specialized breed of mutual funds, supposedly limited to a small group of sophisticated and well-heeled investors who presumably can understand what the fund manager is doing with their money, and can afford to lose it. Some hedge funds require a minimum of $1 million to participate. With such investors, the funds are permitted by regulators to play fast and loose with investor assets, engaging in bewildering activities like short selling (betting that a stock price will fall, not rise), using derivatives (exotic investment creatures whose description and breeding habits would take another book this size to explain), and leveraging (borrowing money to increase the total investment made). Hedge funds are to normal investing philosophies as thoroughbred horse racing is to pony rides.

Through to the crash of 2008, when they were identified as one of the causes of the crash itself, hedge funds appeared to be making money at a pace that ordinary mutual funds and other investments simply couldn't match. Thankfully, the majority of advisors informed their clients that they didn't have enough money to invest in a hedge fund. The more astute advisors would respond by asking clients if they knew what a hedge fund was and how it worked. Almost none did, yet they were initially determined to invest substantial portions of their investment in one because hedge funds were "hot"—and they were "hot" because they appeared to be making some people an enormous amount of money.

Which was true. It is also true that, next to putting your month's salary on the nose of a racehorse or mortgaging your house to buy a truckload of lottery tickets, there are few riskier investments to make than investing in hedge funds.

Ten years before the crash of 2008, Long-Term Capital Management (LTCM), a popular U.S. hedge fund that had scored dramatic earnings in the past, managed to lose US$4.6 billion in less than four months. This was a feat not even General Motors has been able to duplicate. Only the intervention of then–Federal Reserve chairman Alan Greenspan, who authorized a government-backed bailout, averted a potential collapse of the stock market and a likely resulting recession.

LTCM was not alone; it was merely the most dramatic. Other hedge funds collapsed in a similar dramatic fashion, some losing more than half their assets in less than a month. The reason: Hedge funds exploit risk. When the market is rising, leveraging permits hedge funds to score bigger returns, using borrowed money to inflate the assets. When the market drops, short selling* lets managers make money while everyone else is losing money. But no batter hits 1.000 in baseball, no hockey player gets a hat trick in every game, no ice skater lands a quad on every jump, and no fund manager knows where the market is heading with every trade. When hedge funds won, they won big. When they lost, they somehow lost bigger.

I count two lessons about reducing the risk of your portfolio here. One is a dramatic demonstration of the correlation between risk and reward. The other is subtler but also more universal: *Never invest in something you do not understand.* Almost none of those eager Canadians who demanded to put their RRSP or other investments into hedge funds could tell a derivative from a dermatologist.

There's also a corollary: If your advisor suggests an investment vehicle whose nature and operation he or she does not or cannot explain to you, avoid the investment and give serious consideration to avoiding the advisor.

In his excellent book *Sleep-Easy Investing*, Gordon Pape tells the story of a 28-year-old man who decided he knew enough about investing to conduct some day trading with an online broker. Choosing to invest in a diamond penny stock (can you think of a riskier investment?), the man planned to purchase 7500 shares. Due to a slip of a finger on his computer keyboard, he entered 75,000 instead, a blunder that resulted in an $89,000 debit against his bank account instead of the $8900 he had expected. The amount, in his words, "seriously exceeded my net worth."

It's easy to see why. Unemployed for several months, his sole income was an employment insurance cheque. Why would an

---

*For a detailed explanation of short selling and other terms, please consult the Glossary on page 179.

unemployed investment novice risk $8900 on a penny stock? I don't know either.

The rest of his tale unfolded between disaster and farce. Realizing his error, he tried to have the stock purchase reversed. No dice, the brokerage said. But we'll try to sell it for you. The sell order was placed, but there were no buyers for the stock, only sellers. He finally dumped the stock for a few pennies a share, then demanded that the brokerage replace his loss because it failed to recognize that he was unsuitable for buying such a large quantity of the stock. The brokerage, in the parlance of Bay Street, offered to buy him a kite.

You may see this as a classic example of refusing to accept responsibility for one's actions. I would agree, but in this context it's also a lesson in not venturing into areas where your risk vastly exceeds your comprehension.

Control Volatility with the 3-D Approach

You probably don't understand hedge funds, and the Fama-French Three-Factor Formula may look like arithmetic salad to you. Relax. You can control volatility and reduce risk with a variety of tactics, some easier to grasp and practise than others. Start with a 3-D approach, which many find effective—and no, it does not involve sitting in a dark theatre wearing coloured glasses. The three Ds stand for *discipline, diversification,* and *dividends.*

Discipline is the most difficult to learn and apply, and may involve expensive lessons along the way. It requires you to treat your investments as tools. Unless you become sentimental over hammers or toasters, do not become emotional about your mutual funds, stocks, bonds, and other investments.

It also involves contrarian behaviour, which often means not following the herd. This idea appears difficult for many Canadians to grasp, which may explain our reputation as feckless investors. We enjoy being among people who think the same as us. Why should we buy when most others are selling and sell when most others are buying?

Here's why: Because it's a market out there. Sometimes it's a jungle as well, but primarily it's a market, which means that some people understand the true value of whatever is being traded more accurately than others.

Imagine a vegetable market flooded with people selling tomatoes. Now imagine that a blight is beginning to destroy tomato plants throughout the area, but not everyone knows about it yet. Those who possess this knowledge realize that tomatoes will soon not be available from local suppliers, so they buy all they can afford for their own use or to sell at a higher price when the blight hits in full force. The buyers may even pay a premium price for tomatoes, which leads growers who are unaware of the blight to sell every tomato they can pull off the vine.

If you're a tomato seller unaware of the blight, you would probably join the crowd, pleased to sell your tomatoes at the current price. When news of the blight spreads, tomatoes will become scarce, and that's when people who knew the true situation make the big profits.

Or turn it around: Word spreads through the market that a blight is killing tomatoes on farms everywhere in the area. Suddenly everyone wants to stock up on tomatoes, and they begin bidding up the prices, fearing that they will have no tomatoes to eat. Some sellers hoard their tomatoes, hoping the price will rise even higher. A few sellers, however, know that tons of tomatoes will soon arrive from a region where the tomato blight has yet to kill the plants. They sell at the current price before the market is flooded with tomatoes from elsewhere and the price collapses.

In each case, the inexperienced buyer/investor does not know where the risk resides. And in each case, following the herd guarantees a loss of some kind.

Convert those tomatoes into mutual fund units or corporate shares and ask yourself if you would have the courage and discipline to go against the crowd. Without it, the first of the three Ds won't work for you.

Diversification is preached by almost everyone as a wise investment tactic. Applied to investments, it promotes the concept of dividing your money among different industries (agricultural, consumer products, financial services, mining, and so on) if purchasing stocks; it also advises branching out among different sectors and investment philosophies (large-cap, small-cap, precious metals, broad index, global markets, emerging markets/aggressive, conservative, value-based, and so forth).

Dividends represent both a benefit and a guideline when selecting individual stocks for investment. A company with a long record of paying dividends is a stable and profitable operation, generating a stream of income. If a company has never paid dividends, or recently suspended paying them, why bother? Solid companies with a long history of paying reasonable dividends represent a wise investment, and always will.

Can you generate impressive capital gains from companies that do not pay a dividend? Yes, you can. Will two portfolios with dramatically contrasting styles of diversification achieve similar success in controlling volatility? Yes, they might.

Obviously, this isn't a science, and it's something less than an art. "Success" should be defined not by absolutes or ultimates but by acceptability. In this case, it would be acceptable to record losses measurably less than average in a bear market and gains measurably more than average in a bull market. If the market drops 40 percent, which it did in 2008, and your equity (stocks and related mutual funds) portfolio drops 20 percent or less, consider yourself successful. If the markets rise 12 percent annually in a bull market and your equities rise 15 percent, you're successful on the other end.

Here's an easy way to understand concerns over various risks to your RRSP, RRIF, and other portfolios, based on material provided by Keith R. Betty on his *Shakespeare's Investment Primer* website (used by permission):

RISK	HOW TO CONTROL IT
Global Stock Market Crash	Adjust equity/fixed income ratio (less of the former, more of the latter)
One Nation Economic or Currency Crash	Geographic diversification
Sector Crash (metals, industry, etc.)	Limit sector exposure
Company Failure	Limit exposure to a single company
Inflation	Real-return bonds, dividend growth stocks, real estate

With the world still shuddering from the stock market collapse of 2008, investors with substantial RRSP balances whose planned retirement date is within sight are most concerned about a repeat of that disaster.

The solution is *preservation of capital*, which means holding on to whatever you've managed to accumulate so far. While many ways of accomplishing this are available, not all are practical. They include:

High-interest savings accounts. This is the same kind of account your parents probably told you to open as a place to deposit your babysitting earnings or weekly allowance. These accounts were suitable for that; they're not suitable for RRSPs, especially going into the second decade of the 21st century, when they generate about as much interest as last year's Hansard.

Treasury bills. Safe and secure, they're like garages—a good place to park your money, but you wouldn't want to live there. These days, you should avoid them for the same reasons you should avoid savings accounts.

Money-market mutual funds. A place to waste your money by paying other people to put it into treasury bills.

Preferred shares. Owners of preferred shares in publicly traded companies are first in line to receive (usually) fixed dividends, a privilege offered in exchange for not having any shareholder voting rights. They have drawbacks, the most notable being the inclusion of a redemption clause in some preferred shares. Redemption clauses are traps that permit the company to declare, "We're buying back all those preferred shares and using the dividends to lease a new corporate jet," or some other, similar proclamation. This weakens their appeal as a true fortress foundation.

Which leaves bonds.

4

FROM PROPAGATION
TO PRESERVATION

Christopher Cottier leans back in his chair, his hands behind his head. Through the expansive windows behind him, B.C.'s coastal mountains shine in the glow of a late afternoon sun. The frantic pace of distant Bay Street is reflected only in closing market prices from the Toronto Stock Exchange that crawl across his computer monitor, a moving collage of white figures and green and red arrows.

A senior investment advisor with Blackmont Capital Inc., Cottier boasts an interesting blend of university degrees: a BSc in psychology and an MBA. "I find I use the psychology degree more than my business training in assisting clients," he says in his affable British accent. Among the first advisors in Canada to offer non-discretionary fee-based services for small investors, his service (aptly named Liberty) eliminates commissions normally earned from mutual funds, stocks, bonds, and other investments.

He is also gently outspoken in his view of investing for retirement years, disguising his disdain for many industry practices in a warm and jovial manner.

"People get bamboozled when they reach age 70 and realize they have to convert their RRSP savings and investments into an income source," he says.

Too many RRSP owners, Cottier suggests, believe moving from an RRSP to a RRIF must involve a wholesale readjustment of their portfolio. "But it shouldn't. The best plan is to build the portfolio they'll need at age 71, or whenever they decide to move to a RRIF, while they're in their 60s. Then, when you're ready to convert to income generation, most everything is already in place. It's like having a fleet of cars and two different garages. When the time comes, you move all the cars from one garage into the other garage. You have the same vehicles; you just store them in a different place."

Becoming more specific about tactics, he proposes a simple approach to retirement preparation for RRSP owners. During their 60s, he suggests, they should purchase government bonds that mature in the year of their 71st birthday. Then, when government regulations insist they begin withdrawing cash from their (hopefully) fat retirement assets, it's guaranteed to be there in cash.

That's the big question, isn't it? How can RRSP owners in their 40s, 50s, and 60s build maximum assets that permit them to buy all those juicy bonds? There is, of course, no one-size-fits-all solution to maximizing growth in an RRSP portfolio. Much of the decision-making concerns the investor's tolerance for risk, which is always difficult to assess. Cottier, however, suggests a couple of solutions.

"With a married couple, you look at the difference in age between the spouses," he suggests. "I see a lot of second marriages, and often the husband has married someone much younger. If the husband is 55 years of age and his wife is 35, I immediately think in terms of inheritance for the wife because it's clear, or should be, that she is very likely to outlive him by several years."

And if no second marriage or trophy wife (or husband) is in the equation, what then? How can the investor's comfort level be assessed?

Cottier returns to his automobile analogy. "I may ask what kind of car they own, and its age." He smiles, almost conspiratorially. "If the client says it's a ten-year-old Buick, for example, I know I'm dealing with a conservative, low-risk person. If it's a two-year-old Corvette, they're more prepared to ride out some rough weather in search of big gains."

Of course, it's mostly somewhere in between, Cottier explains, but he can usually judge their style with accuracy this way.

Whatever the style, he is not a big fan of Canadian mutual funds. In Cottier's opinion, the fees are too high and the performance is generally unimpressive. Instead of buying units in mutual funds, Cottier suggests, investors might consider buying shares in the mutual fund companies themselves. "If you like the taste of milk," he smiles, "buy a piece of the cow." And don't be greedy. "The average top-quality equity investment delivers about 10 percent average annual return. If you get a year in which you make 20 percent, take your profits and be satisfied."

He has another warning. "Never fall in love with your investments. "Whatever you have in your portfolio, they're not friends or families. They're tools, and if a tool doesn't perform well because it's broken or it's too expensive or there's a better one at hand, toss the old one aside."

All of this, Cottier suggests, is a lead-up to the importance of quality bonds as a means of securing the gains earned over a lifetime of RRSP investing. "Your key goal at retirement," he points out, "is not to focus on growth but to battle taxes and inflation."

Chris Cottier's ability to offer a fee-based, commission-free remuneration style and a holistic approach to retirement investing should be a revelation to RRSP investors who place their financial future in the hands of traditional advisors. Nothing in his style of assessing client needs is by the book, from using an out-of-left-field means of analyzing risk to warning about the risk of growing amorous over certain investments. Perhaps his most succinct and eye-opening advice concerns the idea of purchasing guaranteed bonds* that mature in the year that RRSP investors reach age 71, when their RRSPs must be converted to an income-generating RRIF. The selection of bonds is predicated on the investor having begun contributing to a registered plan in their 40s or earlier, when enough capital has been accrued to make it worth protecting in that manner.

A quick summary of RRSP/RRIF rules is probably appropriate here:

- At the end of the year you turn 71 years of age, you must convert your RRSP to a RRIF or purchase an annuity with the proceeds. This is critical; miss the deadline and Revenue Canada assumes you have cashed out your RRSP making the entire amount taxable, a crushing blow. The firm with which you have your RRSP invested should alert you to the need to convert your account well in advance of the deadline and handle all the necessary paperwork on your behalf. Make no assumptions; ensure that the action is taken.

- A RRIF may hold the same investments as an RRSP, hence Chris Cottier's analogy of moving a fleet of cars from one garage to another.

- The role of the RRIF reverses that of your RRSP. Before age 71, you paid into the RRSP. After age 71, the RRIF pays you.

- RRIF withdrawals from your account must follow a minimum annual schedule (sometimes referred to as minimum annual payout or MAP) based on your age. At age 71, when switching to a RRIF is compulsory, you must withdraw 7.38 percent of your RRIF balance. As of mid-2009 (Ottawa has a habit of

---

*When I speak of government-guaranteed bonds I am referring to strip bonds (more about these later), not Canada Savings Bonds, whose yields are ridiculously low. Give CSBs to your grandchildren if you can't think of anything else for their birthday, but leave them out of your RRSP/RRIF.

tinkering with RRSP/RRIF rules), the minimum withdrawals were as follows:

YOUR AGE	ANNUAL MINIMUM WITHDRAWAL (% OF RRIF)	YOUR AGE	ANNUAL MINIMUM WITHDRAWAL (% OF RRIF)
60	3.33	78	8.33
61	3.45	79	8.53
62	3.57	80	8.75
63	3.70	81	8.99
64	3.85	82	9.27
65	4.00	83	9.58
66	4.17	84	9.93
67	4.35	85	10.33
68	4.55	86	10.79
69	4.76	87	11.33
70	5.00	88	11.96
71	7.38	89	12.71
72	7.48	90	13.62
73	7.59	91	14.73
74	7.71	92	16.12
75	7.85	93	17.92
76	7.99	94 & older	20.00
77	8.15		

- If your spouse is younger than you, you can delay withdrawals until he or she reaches age 71.
- No withholding tax is applied to the minimum withdrawal, but it is applied to any amount above that figure. For example, if the minimum withdrawal amount is $20,000 and you withdraw

$25,000, withholding tax is applied to the $5000 difference. The entire amount, of course, must be included in your income tax return for that year.

- As noted earlier, Ottawa likes to tinker with RRSP/RRIF rules, so always confirm any new status on minimum withdrawals and other regulations before making a decision.

It's Easier to Protect against Losses Than to Recover Them

Bonds are no way to accelerate your retirement savings balance; guaranteed bonds are the best way, however, to ensure that your portfolio can absorb the blow of stock market disasters similar to the one that struck in 2008–2009, and they provide a fixed portion of your assets when you choose to retire. During the decade of your 60s, you should shift the focus of your RRSP strategy from *propagation* to *preservation*, because you have fewer years to earn back major losses.

Compare the following two charts. The first illustrates the number of years needed to recover losses of 35 percent in a $100,000 portfolio, the amount suffered by many RRSP owners whose portfolio was heavily weighted in stocks before the 2008–2009 recession struck.

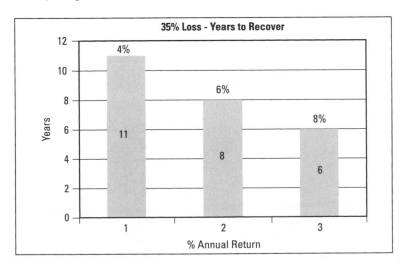

If these investors manage to earn 8 percent annual return on their existing portfolio for six consecutive years, they'll earn back the 35 percent loss suffered from one year of a bear market. An average annual return of 6 percent may be more realistic, in which case they'll need eight years. Remember: This simply returns the portfolio's value to the level it was at in mid-2008, meaning eight years of potential growth has been lost.

Having a larger proportion of their portfolios in guaranteed bonds and other quality fixed income vehicles might have reduced their losses over the same period to 20 percent. So how much time would it have taken to recover in that case?

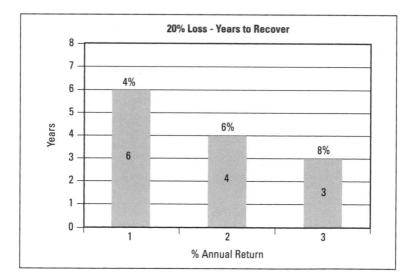

Instead of waiting eight years at a 6 percent annual return, these owners need half the time, compared with those who lost 35 percent in a single year, to reach their portfolio's value before the bear market struck.

A Simple Formula That Works—To a Point

The tried-and-true formula for both growth and preservation of capital is to equate your age with the proportion of your RRSP in guaranteed bonds. At age 65, about two-thirds of your assets should fall into this category. Does this mean steadily increasing the proportion until, at age 80, four-fifths should be guaranteed?

Not necessarily. You may be quite comfortable maintaining the 65–35 split between fixed income (bonds, GICs) and equity investments. If you succeed in reaching 80 years of age in good health, your best option may in fact be to choose an annuity—not a rewarding choice in your younger years but a tempting decision at age 80 when you've exceeded the actuarial tables for longevity. (More on annuities in Chapter 10: Listen Up, All You Baby Turtles!)

However you measure the proportion, quality bonds represent the foundation of your protection against future losses. Unfortunately, few people understand how to implement the process to benefit themselves more than their broker or advisor.

An IOU Made Complex by Time

Of all the investment options available, bonds are the easiest to grasp in principle yet are most often misunderstood in practice.

Think of a bond as an IOU in exchange for a cash advance. If I borrow $100 from you for a month, you would expect some assurance that it will be repaid. If we are lifelong friends, our relationship is your assurance—hey, what are friends for?

Should our friendship not be close, you would expect some other assurance. I could give you my watch for security, for example, but this makes you a pawnbroker of sorts, a role you may not wish to play. So I hand you a piece of paper, confirming the amount of money I owe you, recording the date I will pay it back to you, and indicating how much interest I will add to the original amount as a means of rewarding your trust. We have created a bond.

The date on which I declare to repay you is the day the IOU/bond *matures*. If I repay you $110 in one month's time, that's an effective annual interest rate of 120 percent (12 times 10 percent)—rather high and outrageous. Of course, if I offered the going bond rate as of mid-2009 of 3 percent annually—translated into 0.25 percent for the month, or 25 cents on $100—you'd consider that insulting.

Here's where things grow complex:

Suppose I promise to repay the $100 to you not next month or even next year, but 10 years or even 30 years from now. This is a different ballgame. You have no idea whether either one of us will be around that far in the future or what the buying power of the original $100 plus interest will be. That's a risk you didn't take when you loaned me $100 for a month, and *somebody always pays for risk*. Whatever interest is fair for a one-month loan will be higher for 20 or 30 years because the risk is higher.

Next, instead of waiting 30 years for payment, which at a nominal interest rate of 6 percent (to keep this example simple) annually compounded would balloon the payback for the $100 to more than $600, you would probably prefer that I paid you interest on the loan on a fixed date every six months. You send me a notice every six months and in exchange I send you the agreed-upon semi-annual payment equalling $3 (one-half of the 6 percent annual interest on $100). These notices are attached to the original IOU but are easily clipped off as *coupons*. When all the coupons are gone, the original loan amount remains, which can be redeemed just as the coupons were for the original $100. If I fail to hand over the amount stated on the coupon on its mature date, I have *defaulted* on the bond.

Perhaps the idea of hoarding the IOU and its coupons for 30 years doesn't appeal to you; you'd prefer to have the cash in hand next month, next year, or sometime in the foreseeable future. Maybe I'll agree and buy the IOU back, wiping out my debt to you. But if I'm short of cash and choose to keep making semi-annual interest payments, what's your option?

You sell the IOU to someone else. If this third party doesn't know as much about me as you do, they're taking a bigger risk than you, and once again *somebody always pays for risk*. In this case it's you.

"This IOU is worth about $500 in principal and interest payments," you may suggest to a buyer, "with a guaranteed $100 on maturity. Who will give me $150 for it?"

Probably no one. Someone may offer $75 or $50 for it. They have *discounted* the IOU due to the risk involved. If my name were Bill Gates instead of John L. Reynolds, the discount would be non-existent—who's going to expect Bill Gates to default on a lousy $100—or $100 million for that matter? If the risk of me failing to pay back the loan validates a high annual interest rate, the much-reduced risk of Bill Gates paying it back would mean reduced interest based on reduced risk that he will default on the bond.

If someone pays you $50 for my $100 bond, they have effectively doubled the interest rate earned, from 6 to 12 percent annually ($6 as a percentage of $50 = 12 percent). And if someone pays you $150 for Bill Gates's $100 bond they have reduced the annual interest from 6 percent to 4 percent ($6 as a percentage of $150 = 4 percent).

None of this affects me, or Bill Gates for that matter—a statement I am unlikely to use in any other context involving money. It does not matter to me who owns the bond; when the coupon arrives at my door, I am obligated to exchange it for the agreed-upon cash.

This oversimplified example demonstrates why the price of quality bonds moves opposite to interest rates. If both the bank rate and the rate of a specific kind of bond are identical—let's say they're both at 6 percent—and the bank rate drops to 5 percent, the price to purchase the bond will rise accordingly. Why? Because buyers will find the higher bond rate more attractive than the available bank rate. By paying more for the bond, they will reduce the yield somewhat—see the Bill Gates example above—but still enjoy, they hope, a premium return.

Similarly, if the bank rate jumps to 7 percent, the price of a similarly priced bond on the market will drop because buyers will obtain a higher interest rate by paying less to participate. Bonds, by the way, often move independently of the stock market. A declining stock market may or may not mean a rise in bond prices. Bonds are not the opposite end of the same teeter-totter but a different toy entirely.

One more comment about that risk thing:

All bonds are backed by one kind of asset or another. In my case, I may back it up with my word or my watch. A corporation may back its bond issue with assets; bondholders are usually the first in line if the issuer declares bankruptcy. In Canada, the federal and provincial governments issue bonds galore, all backed by the country or province whose name is on the IOU. Which should help you sleep well.

It's Not All about Protection

Traditionally, the distinction between the role of equities (stocks or mutual funds investing in stocks) and the role of bonds or other fixed income vehicles has been clear and distinct: The former is to build your capital, and the latter is to preserve it. Generally this is true but, like all generalizations, it has exceptions—major exceptions.

Bond returns vary widely with time. Back in 1982, for example, many RRSP investors, including this one, sank a large portion of their portfolios into 10-year bonds issued by Ontario Hydro, the province's electric power-generating and distribution company. Ontario Hydro was as blue-chip as the banks, yet its bonds were yielding 16 percent annually, reflecting the high inflationary environment of the time (home mortgage rates exceeded 20 percent annually in some instances).

Everyone knew that inflation would diminish at some point, but those Hydro bonds would keep paying 16 percent a year (based on their then-current purchase price) until maturity. When inflationary pressures faded and high interest rates dropped to near-normal levels, the price of the bonds skyrocketed, at which point I sold my position for, as I recall, about twice what I had paid just a couple of years earlier. Could I have made 50 percent a year for two straight years from the stock market? Not without taking an enormous amount of risk and counting on an equal degree of luck. The Hydro bonds, remember, were guaranteed by the Province of Ontario; nobody was going to guarantee me a penny on the stock market.

Of course, 1982 was an exceptional year for interest rates. Twenty-five years later, the concept of a guaranteed bond paying 16 percent annually sounded like science fiction. In mid-2009, quality bonds barely nudged 2 percent annually—but whatever the interest rate, the bonds always paid, which is not something you can say about the stock market in the past decade.

ETFs and Strip Bonds: The Game Becomes Exotic

Suppose you and I had $10,000 to invest back in February 2001. You placed yours in a low-cost exchange traded fund (ETF) mirroring the

SOURCE: www.globeinvestor.com. Used with permission.

Toronto Stock Exchange Composite Index.* I, being paranoid about losing money, bought guaranteed bonds and GICs. So where would each of us be in mid-2009?

In November 2002, I would have been gloating. My bonds were up a mere 10 percent or so while your index funds, reflecting the overall Canadian stock market, were *down* by 20 percent. Five and a half years later, in May 2008, you would be laughing at me; your investment had more than doubled while mine was up barely 40 percent.

But look what happened over the next 12 months. At the end of April 2009, our earnings were roughly equal, but I had slept better over the previous year. Much better.

Does this make ETFs a poor choice for an RRSP? Not at all, as we'll discover. Nor does it make every bond a secure and profit-generating choice for investors seeking security. In that instance, look for two qualities in a bond: government-guaranteed, and stripped.

Each coupon on a long-term bond (maturing five-plus years in the future) carries a redemption date, usually every six months for the life of the bond. Normally, the bondholder keeps the entire bond in a safety deposit box, wall safe, or mattress, removes it twice a year, cuts away the coupon bearing that day's date, and exchanges it for cash at a bank or brokerage.

Several years ago, an impatient bondholder had a brilliant idea, probably inspired by a need to pay the rent: Why not clip the coupons now and sell them at a discount? In essence, the bonds were *stripped* of their coupons and sold individually, creating a series of mini-bonds with fixed maturity dates. The price paid for the coupons (called *strip* or *stripped bonds*) would reflect the value on the coupons'

---

*An index can reflect basically the entire Canadian economy (the S&P/TSX Composite Index, tracking all companies listed on the Toronto Stock Exchange); defined sectors of the economy (energy, financials, gold, and so on); or foreign economies and sectors (Dow Jones, NASDAQ, FTSE, Hang Seng, and so on). When judging the performance of a mutual fund or individual investment portfolio, the appropriate index is similar to par in golf—are you over or under it? Exchange traded funds are pools of investments that mimic a defined index. For more on ETFs, see page 80.

maturity date; the price paid and the amount of time between now and then would determine the nominal annual interest.

A strip bond maturing in 10 years when it can be exchanged for $1000 might sell for $600 today. The $400 profit, earned over 10 years, would represent an annual interest yield of 6.66 percent. A $1000 coupon from the same bond maturing 20 years from now and earning the same interest would sell for about $275 to earn 6.66 percent profit until maturity; pay less than $275 for the strip bond and you'll earn more interest.

Strip bonds, especially those guaranteed by the federal or provincial governments, are appealing to conservative RRSP investors for three reasons.

First, they are guaranteed by a stable, democratic government. Few things in life are guaranteed. When you encounter something as good as this, take advantage of it.

Second, they are the only practical method of ensuring that a known amount of money will be available to you at a fixed date. Remember Chris Cottier's tactic of purchasing strip bonds maturing in the year an RRSP owner reaches age 71? There is a good deal of comfort in knowing how much cash you can expect at that point, especially if your RRSP portfolio includes equity investments to provide defence against inflation between now and then.

Third, strip bonds are impractical outside of an RRSP, RRIF, or TFSA thanks to nasty treatment by the Canada Revenue Agency. The folks in the federal tax department have this strange assumption that a strip coupon spits out money annually, like a once-a-year cheque from your favourite aunt. It doesn't, of course; it just sits there like last month's laundry list until its maturity date rolls around.

Doesn't matter. Hold a strip bond outside of a registered portfolio and you'll be taxed each year for the increase in the bond's value, even though you haven't seen a penny's profit. This makes a strip bond held outside an RRSP, RRIF, or TFSA about as popular as a Liberal skunk at a Conservative garden party, which works to your advantage as an RRSP investor. Their unpopularity for non-registered portfolios reduces their appeal and limits the demand, which depresses their price and increases the interest paid.

Traded strip bonds, by the way, are rarely if ever cut from a piece of paper that looks like a royal proclamation. Like other aspects of finance and investment these days, your strip bond exists in cyberspace, its ownership confirmed on your portfolio statement.

What Price Safety?

Someone once defined intelligence as the ability to hold two conflicting ideas at the same time and admit the veracity of both. On the cusp of the second decade of the 21st century, here's a good example: Government bonds are an ideal way of protecting your RRSP portfolio against catastrophic loss, and government bonds are also a lousy investment.

Both are true. With five-year government bonds paying less than 2 percent annual interest, and annual inflation rates hovering around 1.5 percent, you have to ask yourself if this is a good deal. It's not.

Higher inflation rates will be almost unavoidable by 2015, thanks to governments dumping money into the market from great heights and large barrels. When inflation arrives, those 2 percent bond interest rates will be first laughable then tragic, especially if the owners try to sell them before maturity. When interest rates rise to, say, 6 percent or about four times the current rate, the selling price of bonds paying 1.5 percent will fall dramatically in order to boost the nominal rate up to the current market rate. Think of it: You are faced with two competing bonds, both maturing on the same date sometime in the future. One earns you 1.5 percent annually and the other earns you 6 percent annually. Which would you prefer to buy?

Sometimes a Calculated Higher Risk May Be Worth It

Is it possible to slide both security and growth into your portfolio at the same time? Yes, from the private sector, although this will result in more of one (growth) and less of the other (security).

Private corporations have been issuing bonds for centuries. Lamentably, the adjective *junk* has been associated with a certain class of corporate bonds in recent years. Quality corporate bonds are almost as fail-safe as the government species, historically delivering only about 1 percent higher interest than comparable government bonds, indicating that the difference in the risk quotient between the two bonds is thin.

Instead of settling for a laughably low annual interest rate of less than 2 percent from Canadian government bonds in 2009, some Canadians were stuffing their RRSPs and other portfolios with bonds issued by Suncor, with a yield to maturity of more than 6 percent, or a George Weston Ltd. bond delivering around 7 percent through maturity in 2014.

These rates likely won't be around by the time you read about them here, but other bonds are probably available at similar rates from similarly familiar companies. Why? Because, as you may have noticed, one of the most critical impacts of the 2008–2009 credit crisis has been a paucity of capital from traditional sources like investment banks and private lenders. You can also understand why few firms have tried to raise capital through a new issue of common shares. At the same time, corporate bonds caught the same bear market disease that trashed the stock markets, leaving the bonds almost as under-priced as common shares and delivering impressive yields.

"Aha!" I hear you say. "There is no free lunch. I'll be paying for those bigger yields with bigger risk, and that's precisely what I am trying to avoid."

Quite right, but in this case there's a trade-off. We're still talking blue-chip companies here, not mom-and-pop variety stores. If you feel comfortable buying shares in Suncor, George Weston, and similar quality companies, you should feel equally comfortable buying their bonds as well. Your chance of losing from bonds and shares due to corporate collapse is equal, after all. For the record, fewer than 1 percent of all investment-grade corporate bond issuers have defaulted since 1970. I'll take odds of 100+ to 1 in my favour any day.

You can even protect yourself against inflation with bonds, or at least with a specific kind of bond. *Real return bonds* acknowledge something that everyone knows but few people acknowledge, and that's the risk of inflation eating into the value of their mid- or long-term investments. A $10,000, 10-year bond purchased today may put that many loonies in your hand when it matures, but they won't buy as much as 10,000 of them buy today, even at current low inflation levels.

Following the consumer price index (CPI), real return bonds adjust their semi-annual payments in response to inflationary pressures. When the CPI is flat, these bonds are unexciting. Should inflation arrive with a vengeance and drive the CPI to stratospheric levels, as it did in the early 1980s, the bonds pay a bonus to balance the loss in real income.

Real return bonds giveth, but *callable bonds* taketh away. Literally.

Some corporate bonds can be "called," meaning the company issuing them can order you to return the bonds in exchange for money under defined conditions. So you may be resting comfortably against your 10-year bond only to find it yanked out from under you and a bag of cash left in its place.

Bond issuers value callable bonds because they can reduce their debt when interest rates rise (reducing the cost of buying back their bonds, because the bond price drops) or finance new debt at lower annual cost when interest rates fall. A callable bond may include a provision reading, "Callable at 102 after 5 years, declining to par in 9 years." Translation: Five years after distributing the bonds, the issuer could pay you 102 percent of the bond's par value. Should you refuse, the longer you hang on to it, the less money you'll receive.

Nobody likes callable bonds except the issuer, which explains why their price is discounted compared with non-callable bonds. A discounted price means a higher yield, but a callable bond adds an extra layer of risk. Try to avoid them in your RRSP.

Bond Buyers Beware ...

The biggest challenge to most Canadians is not owning bonds, it's buying them. Purchase all the shares you want of Acme Widgets from a financial advisor or online brokerage and you'll know how much you paid, including commission, down to the penny. Buying bonds is like shopping blindfolded in a foreign flea market where you don't speak the language.

Corporate bonds, being less liquid than shares in the company, are not traded in the same volume with the same ease. They're not sold directly in small quantities either, meaning you'll need a broker to make single purchases. Good luck discovering how much the brokerage makes on the deal. The larger the commission, the less you'll earn, but you'll probably have to nag the brokerage to discover just how much of your money they're keeping. This applies to both corporate and government bonds, and irks a lot of people who demand greater transparency in the investment industry.

Before buying a bond from anyone, shop around. Call various brokerage bond traders (yes, they'll talk to you) and ask for their selling price on a stripped bond of a specific maturity date and price ("$10,000 maturing June 2015") and the issuer. You may be surprised at the wide range of prices quoted for the same bond. If dealing with a brokerage-employed advisor, don't hesitate to call him or her and ask for the same bond at the lowest quoted price from elsewhere.

Should You Buy a Bond Fund Instead of a Bond?

Dozens of bond-based mutual funds are available to RRSP investors, most of them with abysmal performance. In the 10-year period from

May 1999 to May 2009, Canadian bond funds delivered an average annual return of 4.26 percent, a hair's breadth better than the index performance of 4.22 percent. On that basis, it's better to own a bond-based exchange traded fund (ETF).

An ETF trades on a stock exchange, generally tracking the performance of an index. It represents a basket of securities reflecting the index and can include stocks, bonds, or other assets. Units or shares can be bought and sold during market trading hours at prices that change throughout the day, and purchased through a full service or discount/online brokerage. Sounds like a stock? Precisely. But in many ways, ETFs are better because they offer built-in diversification, enable you to buy an entire portfolio of securities in a single stock, and generally offer lower volatility, meaning their price will not fluctuate as widely over time.

Bond ETFs deliver three advantages:

1 They're much cheaper to manage. Managers of traditional bond funds slap a management expense ratio (MER) as high as 1.92 percent on the fund unit holders. When the bonds they're buying deliver perhaps 2 percent annually, who's really making money on this deal? It ain't you.

2 They're liquidable, meaning you won't have a problem converting your investment into cash. Strip bonds are easily bought and sold through brokers, of course, but only after the brokerage takes its (usually) hidden commission.

3 ETFs can purchase bonds at a lower price than you can. Lower price means higher earnings.

Bond funds lack the one thing that provides strip bonds their snug comfort: predictability. With a strip bond you know the precise future date and fixed value of your investment. With bond funds, even of the ETF variety, you're not sure.

5

CRISIS-RESISTANT INVESTMENTS: HOW MUCH ASSISTANCE DO YOU NEED TO ACQUIRE THEM?

In 2004, Allison Godden* had had enough. Preparing to retire from her second career as a real estate agent in a small southern Ontario city, she had watched in dismay as the value of the mutual funds in her RRSP continued to dwindle even while the stock market appeared to be edging upwards.

"I really couldn't take the stress of watching twenty years of building my RRSP melt away just as I was finally planning on using it as income," she recalls. So, after consultation with her partner, Allison visited the bank brokerage where her account was registered and took drastic action. "I told them to sell all the funds and put the money in GICs," she says. "Every penny of it."

The bank was aghast. Drop out of the market entirely? Not have any investment at all in equities? Did she really know what she was doing?

She certainly did. "I knew I risked watching stock values rise and hearing other people brag about how much money they were

---

*A pseudonym.

making," she says. "But that wouldn't stress me out nearly as much as worrying if I'd still have enough to live on in a couple of years."

For about two years, Godden's decision remained questionable. Her GICs were earning reasonable rates but not nearly as much as the stock market. Her actively managed equity-based mutual funds had failed to keep pace with the TSX in the past, so this was hardly worrisome. When the market began its slide in early 2008 followed by the major collapse of 2008–2009, however, she felt vindicated.

"No matter what happens to the stock market from now on"— she smiles—"I've got peace of mind and a good night's sleep. And those have their own value to me."

Allison Godden's experience, and the long-term impact it made on her investing philosophy, tap into our latent reaction to the question of risk. Do we abhor it? Welcome it? Exploit it? Avoid it?

Dealing with risk often leads to irrational behaviour by investors— and yes, I mean you (and me, from time to time, but let's not turn this into a mass confessional). The most common example of this is a tendency to buy high and sell low. Basic logic, and every investment book with more words in it than a Rolling Stones song, tells you to do the opposite. Yet every day of the year, investors surveying mutual funds or stock market winners spot a company whose price has soared by a factor of two or three in a short period of time, and they sprint to board the bandwagon. Unfortunately, the bandwagon is usually at the crest of a hill at that point and they ride it down into a valley of losses, screaming all the way.

In explaining the folly of chasing winners only to catch losers, I use the analogy of grocery shopping in a supermarket and passing a display of canned tuna. If a shopper notices her favourite brand of canned tuna has doubled in price over the past week or so, will she slide a few tins into her shopping cart? Not bloody likely. She'll probably switch to salmon or some other substitute until the price drops back to a realistic level. That's rational behaviour.

Reverse the situation: The shopper's favourite canned tuna is now half the price it was last week. Yippee! She loads up with her favourite fish before the price goes back to its normal level. More rational behaviour.

Many investors turn the tale backward, buying into the market at or near peak price before selling with dismay when the price drops through the floor. The behaviour appears even more irrational because recent research indicates investors are so risk-averse that they hate losing more than they enjoy winning.

Think about that for a minute.

We will risk $2 in a national lottery that offers the prospect of winning $10 million. It's easy to toss $2 or $10 away in the face of such tremendous odds in return for the prospect of such a massive return because, among other reasons, no one—including ourselves—will be aware of the loss. As the amount at risk increases, so does our aversion to risk. You may bet $1 with me on a simple coin toss, choosing either heads or tails, for the prospect of walking away with $2 at even odds. Would you bet $100,000 with me on the same gamble, paying the same odds? Probably not, if you're a rational person and not susceptible to a gambling addiction.

Now let's put that $100,000 in your RRSP and assume that you're as risk-averse about it as you were about flipping a coin for the same amount. Someone—your financial advisor, your brother-in-law, a voice in a TV commercial—suggests you put that hundred large into an actively managed mutual fund. The fund manager, your source tells you, makes astute decisions based on extensive research backed by brilliant analysis conducted continuously across the globe, and as a result has generated exceptional returns in the last year, yada yada yada.

Having someone watch over your money minute by minute, making decisions based on data you'll never acquire and probably do not understand, sounds irresistible. And the fund has made enormous gains in the past year? Hey! Where do you send your money?

Now stand back from the slot machine and shake hands with Reality.

You Want Odds? We've Got Odds, and You Won't Like 'Em

A respected study published in the *Journal of Portfolio Management* revealed that over a 10-year period (1989–1998) only 9 percent of actively managed mutual funds in the United States delivered a bigger return than the relative benchmark or index. In other words, the odds were better than 11 to 1 against an investor in a managed mutual fund earning more than someone who bought unmanaged shares in companies listed on an index similar to the fund's.

It gets worse: While the average measure of overperformance by a winning managed mutual fund over the relevant index was 1.8 percent higher, *the average underperformance by a losing managed fund was 4.8 percent.* You were less than 2 percent ahead of the gang if you won and almost 5 percent behind it if you lost—and the odds were 11 to 1 that you would lose. Dividing the underperformance by the overperformance and multiplying by those 11 to 1 odds, researchers measured risk-adjusted odds against beating the index performance at 28 to 1.*

That's fine for U.S. experiences, you may say. But things are different in Canada.

Yes, they are. Our mutual fund costs, measured by average MERs and other fees, are substantially higher than those of U.S. mutual funds or, for that matter, mutual funds marketed anywhere else in the world.

---

*In reality, the odds are even higher because they do not include mutual funds that, because of poor performance, were discontinued or merged with more successful funds during the same period. This reflects the mutual fund industry's practice of concealing evidence of losses by eating their dead.

A highly regarded 2006 study* found total fees for actively managed funds averaged 1.71 percent in the United States and 2.87 percent in Canada. Expensive fees make it difficult for actively managed funds to beat the index, so the odds against success are almost certain to be significantly higher in Canada than in the United States.

An even more devastating study conducted by Morningstar, Inc. and released in May 2009 examined mutual fund operations and regulatory issues in 16 countries around the world, grading them from A to F on various qualities. Canada earned an F on fees and expenses, and the report noted, "Canada's failing grade in fees is the lowest grade received in any of the surveyed areas." It also pointed out:

> Canadian MERs contain "trailer fees,"† which are [annually deducted] fees fairly specific to the Canadian market.... The typical [Canadian] investor pays a front-end load between 4% and 5%, primarily because investors are unaware that this fee is negotiable [with brokers/advisors].... Canadian investors do not pay much attention to fees. Canadian investors are comfortable with the fees because they don't know how low these fees should actually be. Assets tend to flow into average- or higher-fee funds because Canadian investors use financial advisors to help them make decisions. Advisors direct client assets to funds that pay better trailers. And since the trailer is included in the MER, the result is that assets flow into higher-fee funds.‡

Higher MERs are just the beginning of the costs associated with an actively managed mutual fund. Added into the mix are front-end or

---

*Ajay Khoraba, Georgia I.T.; Henri Servaes, London Business School; and Peter Tufano; Harvard Business School, *Mutual Fund Fees Around the World*.

†For more on trailer fees, see page 124.

‡John Rekenthaler, CFA; Michelle Swartzentruber; Cindy Sin-Yi Tsai, CFA, CAIA, *Morningstar® Global Fund Investor Experience*, May 2009.

back-end loads paid to the commission-based advisor who sold the fund, brokerage commissions paid by the fund to do all the trading determined by the fund manager, and those annual trailer fees paid each and every year. With some funds turning over their assets four or more times annually, these commissions can be significant. And whose pockets do you think the commissions are extracted from—the fund manager's or the investors'?

This emphasis on earnings may seem out of place in a book about defensive investing, but it's not. In fact, it's totally relevant, especially to RRSP investors, *because the more you put away in the good times, the less you'll lose in the bad times. Rising stock markets tend to reflect sectors and individual companies with varying degrees of reward for the winners; bear markets are like a blanket that descends upon all and sundry equally.* If the $100,000 equity investment in your RRSP manages to gain 50 percent in a bull market, leaving you with $150,000 (see how easy the math can be?) and I earn merely 40 percent over the same period on my $100,000, what happens in a bear market that chews up 30 percent of our capital? When the dust settles, I'm left with $98,000 ($140,000 minus 30 percent) and you're chuckling with $105,000 ($150,000 minus 30 percent), proving that *maximizing your returns in the good times without altering the risk factor is a strong defence against losses in the bad times.*

Before you dismiss the value of earning only 1 percent more per year from your equity investment as not being worth the effort, check the accompanying chart comparing the growth of $100,000 over 10-, 15-, and 20-year periods at annual returns of 6, 7, and 8 percent.

ANNUAL RETURN	10 YEARS	15 YEARS	20 YEARS
6%	$179,085	$239,656	$320,713
7%	$196,715	$275,903	$386,968
8%	$215,892	$317,217	$466,096

It's easy to shrug off earning 1 percent less than your RRSP might have made in a single year due to high fees on an actively managed mutual fund. It's not so easy when you discover how much it costs you over 10, 15, or 20 years. If I had been shrewd enough to generate 7 percent annually over 20 years and you were content with 6 percent over the same period, my original $100,000 would now be worth almost $67,000 more than yours.

Time to Go Home: The Traditional Mutual Fund Party May Be Over

If I were the manager of a large and successful mutual fund these days, I would have a lot of wealth and a lot of worries, although enough of the former tends to alleviate much of the latter.

It's taken a good deal of time, but Canadians are beginning to understand that the best way to become wealthy is not by purchasing units in a mutual fund, but by owning and managing the fund itself. That's because Canadian mutual fund expenses charged to those who entrust the fund with their money are outrageously and indefensibly high. The mutual fund industry may sputter and groan about higher administrative costs in Canada, claiming such culprits as the need for bilingual documentation, but when was the last time you heard about a tag day to raise money for destitute mutual fund operators? Canadian mutual funds charge excessive MERs and other fees because they *can*, not because they need to.

As a means of providing novice investors with a small asset base (less than $20,000) and a long-term horizon (at least 10 years), a carefully selected mutual fund may be a good choice if costs are low and the management's ethics are high. This is a difficult combination to track down. High MERs and sales commissions paid by mutual funds (and we know where the money to cover theses costs originates, don't we?) create a drag on performance that can negate even a brilliant manager's investment acumen. Commissions paid to brokers, advisors, and mutual fund salespeople are not a drain on the MER but a separate expense deducted from the fund before the fund's unit holders are paid.

Since mutual funds are spending their investors' money in these trades, you might expect them to make the information available to interested unit holders. You might also expect to see winged hogs in the sky too.

Dan Hallet, a highly regarded consultant to the Canadian mutual fund industry, asked several companies whether he could examine their statement of portfolio transactions, or STPs, to gain an understanding of their procedures. Every mutual fund company turned him down flat, even when he offered to sign a confidentiality agreement to prevent disclosure. Such data, the funds responded through their legal counsel, was non-public (does that mean "private"?) information and could not be revealed.

Hallett correctly labelled this reply nonsense. "There's no compelling reason to keep this data secret," he wrote in an industry trade publication. "Mutual funds trade at net asset value, and old trading data cannot possibly influence any mutual fund's market price or NAV."* He also wondered how much of a mutual fund manager's own investment assets were entrusted to the funds they managed. The near-universal response: a significant amount, indicating the managers believe their own counsel. No one, however, volunteered percentages. If a fund manager held 90 percent of his or her RRSP assets in the fund he or she managed, wouldn't you feel better about having your money in their care? How would you feel if it was just 40 percent? Or 10 percent?

You may give as much thought to your mutual fund's STPs or the manager's own trust in the fund's performance as you do to the colour of the prime minister's socks. That's fine. But you should be aware that

---

*Dan Hallett, "A Regulatory Wish: Fixing These Problems Would Make Life Better for Investors," *Investment Executive*, May 5, 2009.

the companies that badger you with their low opinion of your ability to handle your RRSP investments prefer, in almost every aspect of their operations, that you avoid asking embarrassing questions such as "How do you spend the money I pass along to you?" and "What do you do to earn the management fee you charge?"

Publicly traded mutual fund companies also face a rarely discussed serious conflict of interest in their decision-making: They have a primary fiduciary obligation to their stockholders, not to their investors. When this occurs, as David Swenson reports in his book *Unconventional Success: A Fundamental Approach to Personal Investment,** this relationship "inevitably resolves in favour of the bottom line." If it's a matter of making money either for the mutual fund's stockholders or for the people whose money the fund manages, the stockholders win every time. See why it can be more profitable to invest in the mutual fund company than in the mutual fund itself?

Thanks to the enormous marketing power of mutual funds, most Canadians are drawn to the largest funds managed by the largest fund companies. This creates a sense of safety—but let's remember that the *Titanic* was a pretty big boat.

Here's a revelation: *The bigger a mutual fund grows, the more it resembles an index fund—and why pay somebody 2 or 3 percent of your investment every year for something that you can manage yourself?*

The bigger the fund gets (and the more companies that comprise the fund), the less the manager can pay attention to details. Eventually, management of the fund is handed to a committee and all committees do one thing very well: They cover their collective asses by making middle-of-the-road decisions. Few committees boast rebels who will break from traditional thinking, and soon the fund will begin losing the distinctive characteristics that made it successful. Eventually, the fund becomes a closet index fund, proclaiming its "unique and dynamic approach to seeking out investment opportunities overlooked

---

*New York: Simon & Schuster, 2005, p. 92.

by other funds," which is balderdash when committee-think drives the fund to making the same investment decisions as everyone else.

The smartest person I met in the investment industry was a man named Robert Krembil. In 1981, he and Arthur Labatt, from the brewery family of the same name, launched Trimark Investment Management Inc., which proved to be one of the major success stories in the Canadian mutual fund industry. One of Trimark's operating philosophies, Krembil told me in 1988, was to limit the number of companies it would include in its portfolio to 40. "That's as many as we can track accurately and with confidence," he said. "If we find a company to invest in that's better than any of the 40 already in our existing portfolio, we take out the weakest and insert the new one."

Through the latter part of the 1980s and into the 1990s, few mutual funds in Canada outshone Trimark in performance or prestige. The more it succeeded, the more it attracted new investments. Money poured in, ballooning the fund's assets until it became impossible not only to restrict the portfolio to 40 companies but for Krembil to exert his investment magic. New Trimark funds were launched in an effort to spread the incoming money around, managed by new managers and decisions by committee.

By the late 1990s, Krembil's winning formula was no longer applicable. In 2000, Krembil and Labatt sold Trimark to British-based Amvescap PLC, operator of AIM funds. AIM became a division of Invesco, a gigantic U.S. company managing $350 billion in total assets. A few years later, Invesco dumped the AIM identification and inserted Invesco ahead of Trimark, which bolstered the egos of Invesco executives in Houston and confused the hell out of loyal Trimark investors in Canada.*

So where's the Krembil philosophy that thousands of Canadians (including me) responded to in the glory days of Trimark? Check the

---

*For more on the sad demise of Trimark, see Chapter 7: Fees, Commissions, and Other Holes in Your Bucket.

wastebaskets and paper shredders at Invesco's head office in Houston, Texas. Nothing about the investment philosophy of Trimark today resembles the proven genius of Krembil's approach.

When Everybody Thinks the Same Way …

In May 2009, I surveyed six of the largest mutual funds investing primarily in Canadian equities—the kinds of funds that many financial advisors suggest to their RRSP clients. Here they are with the total assets each fund managed at the time:

COMPANY	FUND	ASSETS	MER
AGF	Cdn Large Cap Classic	$2,040,000,000	1.80%
BMO	Equity Fund	$1,467,000,000	2.28%
Fidelity	Cdn Asset Fund	$3,353,000,000	2.17%
RBC	Cdn Equity Fund	$3,360,000,000	1.96%
TD	Cdn Equity Fund	$1,934,000,000	2.07%
Trimark	Select Cdn Growth	$1,726,000,000	2.34%

SOURCE: www.globeinvestor.com. Used with permission.

Notice that these six funds—not the fund companies, but the individual funds themselves—represent almost $14 billion in cash, most of it entrusted to the fund managers by RRSP owners seeking to build assets for their retirement years.

When I noted the 10 largest holdings of each fund, representing the core of its investment philosophy, the same company stocks, and even the proportion of each company in the top 10 listings kept showing up. Here they are with the number of funds that held them in the top 10 percent of each fund's assets:

Manulife Financial	6
Royal Bank	6
TD	6
Encana	5
Goldcorp	5
Nexen	5
Potash Co. of Canada	5
Research In Motion	5
Suncor	4
Shoppers Drug Mart	2

All the above firms are excellent choices for long-term Canadian investments, but do you or I have to pay MERs of 2 or 3 percent for the privilege of investing in them? And how much real difference can there be between large funds if their holdings are similar?

Here's another problem faced by large mutual funds: Manage a mutual fund with $100 million in assets, and most trades you make on behalf of investors will have all the impact on the market of a hungry mosquito on a sleeping hippo. Selling 2 percent of the fund's holdings, even if just one stock is represented, and buying an equivalent amount of another stock to replace it represents a mere $2 million each way. Should the fund grow to $1 billion in assets, however, a 2 percent trade represents $20 million each way, enough to stir a response on the TSX.

The larger mutual fund could not likely purchase $20 million of stock in one buy, so the money would sit looking for sellers until the purchase was completed. Word would spread about the large buy being made, and prices would rise to meet the existing demand. In effect, the fund would soon be bidding against itself, paying more for the stock than it should. Even if it tried to fill the position with ten buys of $2 million each, the effect on the price would be the same, heightened by bandwagon jumpers bidding the price up.

A similar effect works going the other way. When the fund decides to get out of the same 2 percent of another stock, how does it do so without depressing the price and lowering its return for investors? The word would soon spread—"XYZ Fund is dropping Acme Widgets!"— and many would panic, selling their shares and depressing the price. These are two very good reasons why large mutual funds have difficulty beating the returns of broadly based index funds.

The Good News: You're in Charge of Your Financial Future. The Bad News: You're in Charge of Your Financial Future

You don't have to count on traditional mutual funds to represent the equity portion of your RRSP or other investment portfolio. You can do it yourself. Honest.

A few years ago, I equated successfully managing their own investment portfolio, for most Canadians, with removing their own appendix—it probably can be done, but do you really want to try it?

Things have changed, as they always do. I suspect Canadians are marginally better informed on investment basics than they were a few years ago, thanks to broader and more accessible media coverage. What's more, the economic carnage of 2008–2009 demonstrated that no one has a truly foolproof means of avoiding losses, just as no one has a similar method of guaranteeing better-than-average returns year after year. The recent growth of indexed exchange traded funds (ETFs), offering broadly based investment with minimal expenses and maximum liquidity, reflects this growing attitude. Why pay somebody to do the things you can do yourself for (almost) free?

The time may have come for you to seriously consider managing your own portfolio. It's cheaper, easier, and, with a few cautious steps, safer than a few years ago, thanks to ETFs.

A decade ago, ETFs were as rare as socialists at the TSX; by mid-2009, more than 100 ETFs were vying for Canadian investor attention. Originally aimed at broader indices such as the S&P/TSX Composite, reflecting every company listed on the Toronto Stock Exchange, ETFs now deliver a dozen or more sector choices, including gold, energy, dividends and income, oil sands, natural gas, and maybe even pistachio. Their performance varies according to that of the sector they emulate. No manager is at the helm trying to exceed the index in good times and cushion the fall in bad times, so wherever the sector leads the ETF will follow. In good or bad times, however, the low cost of the ride represents a benefit.

Barclays iShares CDN LargeCap 60 Index ETF boasted total assets of $8.357 billion in mid-2009, invested in many of the same companies as the six actively managed funds shown earlier, including Royal Bank, Encana, TD Bank, Barrick Gold, Goldcorp, Potash Company, Research In Motion, and others. The iShares MER is just 0.17 percent, less than one-tenth the MER of the AGF Canadian Large Cap Dividend Fund Classic, the cheapest fund in the actively managed group.

If you believe in buying and holding over the long term, the most effective method is via ETFs reflecting major sectors of the Canadian stock market. These include the TSX Composite Index; the TSX Large Cap Index (investing in the 60 largest companies on the TSX); the S&P 500 Index (for the largest U.S. companies); and the Canadian Financial Sector Index (banks, investment firms, and insurance companies).

Actively Managed ETFs: An Oxymoron

After years of claiming, with little hard-nosed proof, that an active manager charging an annual MER of 2 percent or more will outperform an ETF with an MER of 0.35 percent for the same period, some actively managed mutual funds are joining the enemy. Well, almost.

In May 2009, Manulife Mutual Funds announced with great fanfare that it was launching three funds based on Canadian, U.S., and international equity indexes, essentially three different ETFs. Very nice. Except that you could not purchase them as stand-alone funds. You could invest in them only with one of Manulife's Simplicity wrap accounts. As much as 20 percent of a Simplicity wrap account's assets could be in the firm's in-house indexed account.

Here's the rub: The Simplicity wrap accounts charge an annual MER ranging from 2.25 to 2.85 percent. Remember what MER stands for: management expense ratio, the fee paid to fund managers in return for their energy and expertise at actively managing the fund's assets, which, of course, consists of your money. Perhaps 20 percent of the investment assets in these Simplicity wraps is now spent passively, tucked into a corner out of the manager's sight while he or she focuses on other things. ETFs such as those marketed by Barclays and others, mirroring the same indices as those employed by Manulife, carry MERs as low as 0.20 percent annually.

So the Manulife Simplicity fund managers are doing 20 percent less work. Is Manulife charging a 20 percent lower MER? Only the naive expect them to do so.

In mid-2009, the Bank of Montreal launched four ETFs with great fanfare, bringing the number of ETFs available in this country to more than 100. BMO was not the first Canadian bank to give ETFs its blessing. TD pioneered the idea in 2001, dropping the funds five years later because they failed to achieve critical mass, which means there were insufficient numbers of units in circulation.

Remember that one of the key appeals to ETFs, besides their very low MERs, is their liquidity—the ability to trade fund units as quickly and easily as shares in public companies. A million or so units in circulation are required to generate buy-and-sell action at competitive market prices, and liquidity becomes difficult if insufficient numbers of units are available. It took TD five years to realize their ETFs would not achieve critical mass. It may take as long for BMO and investors to determine whether the new ETFs promise a longer and more profitable life.

Should You Assemble a Portfolio of Individual Stocks? Well, Yes and No ...

Some Canadian investors are so jaded by mutual fund performance that they are seriously considering what was once unthinkable: bypassing mutual funds entirely and building a basket of stocks on their own. Is this a good idea?

The problem is diversification, which, along with quality fixed income elements such as guaranteed bonds and laddered GICs, represents a bulwark against overwhelming loss. But how many stocks does it take to minimize portfolio loss? Some people claim 15 or 20. Many believe it takes 40. Others, such as investment guru and author William Bernstein, snort at the very idea of fewer than 500.

In a published study titled *The 15-Stock Diversification Myth*, Bernstein claims that over 28 years, from 1980 to 2008, all of the gains reported on the NYSE and NASDAQ were recorded by the top 25 stocks; the remaining 75 percent recorded losses. On that basis, the odds are 3 to 1 against success should you choose a portfolio by throwing darts at the complete stock listing.

You wouldn't do that, of course. You would carefully ponder the future of specific industries, examine past performance of selected companies, weigh this against future prospects, and make your decisions in a methodical manner.

Very nice. But how would you identify companies that Bernstein calls "Super Stocks," names such as RIM or Potash or Dell or Walmart, companies that achieve massive gains, propelling their indices to extraordinary heights well beyond any expectation? You likely wouldn't.

Bernstein focused his attention on the U.S. stock market, about 30 times bigger than the Canadian stock market in total assets, so the universe is considerably smaller in this country. While his theory applies to a similar degree to Canada, it should be subject to modification.

Consider technology, for example. Bernstein mentions Dell as a Super Stock, and it clearly qualifies. He could also have mentioned, in their earlier incarnations at least, Microsoft, Cisco, Sun, Oracle, HP, and at least a dozen other large-cap technology-based companies that qualify. In Canada we have one: RIM.

Here's another difference: No one of consequence is promoting the idea of investing in U.S. financial organizations in 2010, except on a speculative basis. Canadian banks, however, represent a buttress of stability with reasonable prospects of growth and an impressive record of dividend payments. But no Canadian bank can deliver Super Stock performance to the degree that Citibank may or may not. Royal, TD, Scotiabank, and the rest are attractive at least as much for their dividend records and stability as for their growth prospects. Let's face it— assembling a portfolio of stocks in this country means opting for the dull and steady over the wild and risky. Hey, isn't that the Canadian Way?

So consider this strategy: Choose broadly based ETFs as a foundation of your equities spiced with selected individual stocks. Annually, or whenever you achieve a targeted gain in the sector stocks—say 50 percent—plan to rebalance the sector. Reaching a targeted gain of 50 percent might trigger selling one-third of the sector, reducing the level to your original investment, and moving the gain into the fixed-income portion of your portfolio. In the terminology of the market this is known as *crystallizing* your gains.

Subject to the unpredictable vagaries of the stock market and the world in general, here are some guidelines in building a stock portfolio for an RRSP. These are suggested content only; the balance between them is up to you.

1 **If you can't beat the banks, buy 'em.** Through 2009, Canadian politicians and their banking buddies delighted in quoting U.S. President Barack Obama and others on the stability of our banking system. Various international sources called it the best banking system in the world, which considering the state of global banks at the time was like being named the best hockey player in Hawaii.

Still, Canada's banks are solid and profitable, two qualifications for any investment choice. We can complain about their fees, their size, their clout, and their encroachment into other activities besides banking, but bank shareholders in recent years can't complain about their performance. In fact, given their comparable strength TD, Scotiabank, and Royal Bank may be poised for substantial foreign expansion via acquisitions, providing a wider base for potentially larger profits. "Investing in bank stocks," says a market-savvy friend, "is like owning a casino." Not quite, but close.

2 **What's so bad about boring?** Energy stocks are exciting things. If oil hits $200 a barrel, the cheers in Calgary will be heard all the way to Newfoundland. Of course, if it sinks below $40 a barrel, the Alberta oil sands project risks becoming the world's largest junkyard. To avoid the rough ride, bypass the risky and invest in the boring, namely pipeline companies that carry the stuff at any price to consumers. These include Enbridge and TransCanada Corp. Utilities such as Canadian Utilities (CU) are just as boring (even the company's name is dull). CU, part of the Alberta-based ATCO Group, transports electricity and water, generates electric power, and provides global technological services on power generation and related activities. None of these companies is likely to produce major capital gains, but they have low downside risks and long histories of paying fat dividends.

3 **The more cash, the better.** Invest in companies that already have a lot of cash and appear to attract it in truckloads. Loblaws, the country's largest grocery chain; Jean Coutu, a chain of drugstores in Quebec and the Atlantic Provinces; and Alimentation Couche-Tard, with more than 5000 convenience stores across North America, all deal in cash and consumer goods. The latter quality is especially attractive in tough economic times, when people forsake Rolexes and 20-year-old Scotch but still need corn flakes and Aspirin.

4 **All that glitters just might** ... Imagine a product that has been priced artificially low for years, faces a growing worldwide demand for its dwindling supply, and is almost as liquidable as cash. Would you invest in it? You probably can't wait. But perhaps you should.

It's gold. For years, a highly vocal minority of investors and advocates across North America has been predicting that gold is certain to reach $2000 per ounce based on a category of reasons (in mid-2009, the price floated around $1000).

Gold bugs claim governments constantly manipulate the metal's price because a rise in gold prices translates into a decline in the value of national currencies, underpricing gold and overpricing the dollar, pound, euro, and other loose change. Meanwhile, future demand for gold will grow with the expansion of the middle classes in India and China, cultures with good historical reasons for valuing the unquestioned security of gold over promises-backed paper money. The price of gold tends to track the price of petroleum; if oil resumes its position above the $100-per-barrel price, gold is certain to rise alongside it.

Inflation is another booster of gold prices. With governments printing money as though it's cheap wallpaper, inflationary pressures may become inevitable within the next few years, driving the price of gold up to and beyond that $2000 level. Or not.

So, is gold a risk or a refuge? It may be both—a hedge against inflation if held as bullion (or the equivalent), and an astute investment as shares in established gold producers such as Barrick and Goldcorp. Or not.

5 **Go on the defensive.** In downtimes, consumers stop buying plasma TVs and new clothing, but they still need to eat and, in their later years, take medication. Companies providing these goods and the services that accompany them are neglected in boom times and beloved in bad times, providing some protection against downtime disaster. These include George Weston and Loblaws in the food area, and Shoppers Drug Mart in the pharmacy trade. The latter may be a growth stock in the coming few years as boomers find Viagra and Celebrex more tempting than Hugo Boss and Chanel.

6 **Telecommunications could be a new staple.** Older boomers scoffed at the younger generation's passion for cell phones and the gizmos they propagated. Who needed MP3 music files, cameras, video games, text messaging, internet access, and other paraphernalia? It's only a telephone, right?

Wrong. Wireless communication changes more than the way we keep in touch; it is changing the way we live, especially for those under 40. Landline telephones are doomed. Mobile connectivity is becoming a 24/7 service necessity. And if you think RIM has exhausted the market for BlackBerrys, think again: About 2 billion people around the world will become prospective BlackBerry consumers in the next decade, all of them purchasing wireless communication services to use the little devils. It's difficult, on a global basis, to find any industry matching this one for both growth and stability.

6

PAYING FOR "EXPERT" ADVICE THAT PROFITS THE OTHER GUY

In 1995, Ray and Sheila Beauchamps,* a Nova Scotia couple in their mid-50s, earned a combined annual income of $55,000. Their children grown and gone from their mortgage-free home, the couple, both employed in retail, were enjoying the benefits of a frugal, though comfortable lifestyle—no debt, almost $300,000 in RRSPs, and a large brokerage account financed by an inheritance. The assets in their RRSPs were divided 60/40 in shares of blue-chip companies and guaranteed bonds.

When the financial advisor who had worked with them for more than a decade chose to retire, they approached a new brokerage in response to an advertising campaign, explaining that their investment objectives were to obtain an equal balance of income and capital gain from their portfolios.

The new advisor and brokerage recorded neither the level of risk tolerance for the Beauchamps, nor the time horizon they sought. More unsettling, the firm opened a margin account for them, allowing the couple to employ a high-risk leveraging strategy by borrowing against their investments. The Beauchamps agreed to the

---

*Pseudonyms. Source of case study at www.obsi.ca.

strategy, relying on the advisor's assurance that it met their needs, even though they did not understand leveraging or appreciate the risk it represented.

Within a few years, all their RRSP accounts were in high-MER equity-based mutual funds and the income-generating portion of their portfolio had been liquidated to cover interest on the margin expenses. Many of the equity investments were high risk. Meanwhile, their account balance had shrunk to about half its original size.

Dismayed at the results, the Beauchamps asked the brokerage to compensate them for at least a portion of their losses. When the company rejected their claim, the Beauchamps were referred to the Ombudsman for Banking Services and Investment (OBSI), dedicated to resolving disputes between participating banking services and investment firms and their clients. Completing its investigation, OBSI recommended that the couple receive almost $60,000 in compensation, covering only a portion of their losses; the brokerage agreed.

The Beauchamps, not surprisingly, now deal with a different brokerage and advisor, and manage the remnants of their portfolio with a good deal more caution.

Ray and Sheila Beauchamps were fortunate. Few investors recover anything from lost assets as a result of bad investment advice, and the road leading to even a limited settlement tends to be long, winding, and rough.

Financial advisors and their employers battle ferociously to defend themselves against client claims of malfeasance and outright fraud.* Even in cases where the industry's regulator has decreed that the

---

*For a detailed examination of the investment industry's tarnished record of response to client complaints of poor or misleading investment advice, see my book *The Naked Investor: Why Almost Everybody But You Gets Rich on Your RRSP* (Toronto: Penguin, 2005).

advisor or broker was at fault and imposed penalties, the investment firms may refuse to discuss compensation, claiming the investors are "authors of their own misfortune"—this from an industry that decrees most investors are not qualified to manage their own portfolios and, thus, need professional consultation and management.

Yet few qualified professions set lower qualifications for entry. Scoring a 60 percent average on a course examination approved by the Canadian Securities Institute, offered by community colleges across the country, wins you a licence as a mutual fund salesperson and begins the process of qualification to sell other securities. No apprenticeship is required, no residencies are involved, and no articling exists. As a result, there is no formal requirement to observe and interact with experienced individuals who may provide guidance and establish standards of behaviour. Should we be surprised that, as one legal advocate of investor rights has said, "There are some excellent financial advisors out there, those who go through a planning process, who disclose risk. They're excellent and they're a really important part of our economy and our community. Problem is, they're a very small minority."*

The Risk of Making Your Own Decisions versus the Risk of Dealing with "Experts"

The differences between advisors and clients can be measured by the industry's dependence on sales commissions as a source of immediate income; on receiving future income via mutual fund trailer fees; and on maximizing overall income via larger commission payments in return for bigger sales volumes. Even when investors are aware of these

---

*Harold Geller, "The Hired Guns: 'Problem is people finding us,'" *The Globe and Mail*, April 21, 2009.

aspects of the business, they agree with proposed strategies often inappropriate for their needs. How can this happen?

In March 2009, Gregory Burns, a neuroeconomist—now there's an academic specialty for you—at Emory University in Atlanta, Georgia, conducted a series of experiments to measure the brain responses of subjects making decisions on their own and with the assistance of an "expert."*

The process involved tracking blood flow in the subjects' brains while the subjects evaluated near-certain rewards and risky gambles. The first series of tests, permitting the subjects to make decisions on their own, activated two distinct areas of the brain. One region began measuring the payoff, and the other measured the risk, essentially triangulating the measure of loss and gain to reach a verdict favourable to the subject.

When subjects were asked to reach a decision based on the advice of "experts," however, the normally activated parts of the brain remained quiet. None of the purposeful logic seen in the first test was evident, even when the "expert" proffered bad advice. In essence, the "expert" assumed the role of the subject's brain.

Burns called this process "off-loading"—letting the expert do the work your own brain would normally perform. "Your decisions are being driven by the [expert's] advice, not by your own valuation structures," Burns explained. The lesson is clear: The act of seeking an expert's opinion may erase your own opinion. And if you remain unaware of the motive imbalance between you and the commission-paid expert, who seeks immediate and measured reward versus your delayed and indeterminate gain, you are at a severe disadvantage. "You should beware of people offering advice not only because they might be wrong," Burns concluded, "but because [that advice] may inhibit your ability to form judgements."

---

*Jason Zweig, "This Is Your Brain on Investment Advice," *The Wall Street Journal*, March 31, 2009.

A Convoluted Trail That Often Leads Nowhere

When an advisor's proposals and actions cost clients dearly, they discover themselves wandering across a desert of mirages and disappointments. All the smiling faces, firm handshakes, and promises of expert assistance evolve into cold shoulders and legalese.

The standard procedure unfolds thus:

Clients with concerns about their investment portfolio are told to raise them with their advisor. If their advisor cannot satisfactorily respond, they must turn to either their advisor's supervisor or the appropriate compliance officer. The unfolding trail, if the dealer or brokerage rejects their complaints (and it usually does) may lead to the firm's ombudsman or someone appointed to fill that role. This may give the investor a sense of comfort, but it shouldn't. In too many cases, the ombudsman's office is not a sanctuary but a trap.

A client's detailed discussion with a supposedly neutral ombudsman provides the investment firm with confidential information from the complainant, who usually is not accompanied by legal counsel. The ombudsman is employed, after all, not by clients but by the brokerage or investment firm. The firm can and will use any information provided to the ombudsman in the firm's defence, turning the investors' own words against them where appropriate. Moreover, the firm has neither an obligation nor an incentive to reveal similar details of its operations and its advisors' actions to the client. This is a highly stacked deck, enabling brokerages and investment firms to dismiss many legitimate claims with impunity and perhaps even sympathy, but rarely with a satisfactory settlement.

Clients who retain enough energy to keep battling may seek legal assistance at this point. The decision often leads them into a Kafkaesque world where counsel demands a five-figure retainer fee plus monthly charges to pursue a case that is almost certain never to go to court and rarely, if ever, produces an adjudicated settlement of more than a fraction of the lost assets.

Should the advisor or brokerage be a participant in OBSI, the possibility exists for a settlement of some kind, but the odds remain against the investor. Of 346 investment complaint files opened by OBSI in 2008 only 64, or fewer than 20 percent, resulted in a recommendation for funds to be paid to the client. In 103 cases, OBSI sided with the investment firm or advisor.

The odds are even stacked against investors being aware of the procedure; OBSI's own statistics reveal that 6 out of 10 complainants to OBSI had not been told, by OBSI-participating firms, of the dispute regulator's existence when the two sides could not reach agreement.* When investors eventually learned of OBSI's existence and services, they also discovered that the ombudsman is limited to settlements under $350,000 and that the service has no direct authority to force offenders to settle according to its recommendations. You cannot, by the way, approach OBSI until you have exhausted all the means for settlement at one of its member firms which means, if the firm employs an ombudsman, you will have already made statements on the record that could weaken your case.

Should you defy the odds and win, OBSI's only means of enforcing its rulings against participating firms is via publicity, the thinking being that investment companies depending on a positive public image will choose to avoid appearing as deadbeats if they fail to comply. This usually works. But not always, as clients of Financial Architects Inc., a Toronto mutual fund dealer, demonstrated in May 2007.†

The case involved a 76-year-old widow whose monthly income consisted of a $179 pension, CPP payments, and OAS benefits. Her home mortgage-free, she owned a RRIF with a balance of $142,000 invested in medium-risk income and equity mutual funds, set up by

---

*This and other OBSI statistics were obtained from the *OBSI 2008 Annual Review.*
†OBSI News Release: *Mutual Fund Firm Refuses OBSI Recommendation*, May 10, 2007.

a financial advisor. When the advisor left his previous firm to join Financial Architects in the summer of 2000, a substantial portion of the woman's RRIF was shifted to high-risk (and high MER) mutual funds; by the fall of 2000 all of her assets were in equity investments, of which at least 60 percent were considered high risk, leaving nothing for income generation. The client could obtain income only by redeeming units of highly volatile DSC-based equity funds during a declining market, meaning she lost money through both declining values of the units and substantial penalties imposed on her by the DSC funds.

By 2003, the mandatory annual RRIF withdrawals based on the woman's age had declined from more than $10,000 to less than $5000, reflecting a drop in the RRIF's value of more than half within three years.

In a news release, OBSI ombudsman David Agnew commented, "This unsophisticated investor was relying on her advisor. There is no evidence to suggest that any strategy was explained to her, and we do not believe she was aware of the downsides she faced with this risky advice. Leading a widow in her late 70s living on a limited income into a portfolio containing 60-per-cent high risk mutual funds with DSCs is simply unacceptable."

He went on to note that the investments were unsuitable, the strategy ill-conceived, and the firm's recording-keeping "unhelpful," adding, "Financial Architects Inc. could not produce any kind of Know-Your-Client form either on account opening, when the account was transferred, or any other time. Nor could we find a written investment plan. The advisor's notes were spotty at best." OBSI was not persuaded by Financial Architects that the client understood the possible negative consequences of being invested entirely in equities and for the most part in high-risk mutual funds. It recommended that the elderly client receive compensation of $79,797.

Financial Architects responded with an offer to pay the client $248.50 in tax penalties for excess foreign content and $180.86 toward DSC fees.*

OBSI's only rejoinder was to publicize the case and attempt to embarrass the firm into agreeing to the negotiated settlement. Financial Architects refused, resigning from OBSI and a year later resigning from the Mutual Fund Dealers Association. The firm's president (and compliance officer, raising questions about conflict of interest) dissolved the firm. In mid-2009, the same individual was managing a new investment firm operating out of the same offices and with the same telephone number as Financial Architects Inc.

You Are the Last Defence

The widow's experience is unusual because of the refusal of Financial Architects to comply with OBSI's ruling. Similar incidents, in which clients fail to recover any losses at all, are reported on an almost daily basis among investor advocates and, to a lesser degree, in the trade and consumer press. When they occur, investors discover that the investment industry, eager to attract them with promises of future wealth, is swift to reveal that, while the investors and the industry (via MERs, fees, and commissions) will share the upside, only the client pays on the downside. And only the industry can boast favoured organizations to support its position, none of them interested or equipped under any circumstances to enforce the return of lost funds even when the misconduct of advisors has been proven and unchallenged.

Let's be fair here: Investors have to begin accepting a share of responsibility for actions that produce major asset losses. In cases of outright

---

*OBSI news release, *Mutual Fund Firm Refuses OBSI Recommendation,* May 10, 2007.

theft and fraud, the primary error committed by the investor may be one of granting the advisor or broker too much trust. At some point, the question of trusting too much becomes a matter of caring too little. Claims made by investors in response to queries about the client's assets and investment knowledge too often reflect an attempt by the investor either to conceal his or her ignorance about the subject or boast of an inflated asset base.

These fictions usually occur when completing the Know Your Client (KYC) form or Risk Questionnaire, the investment industry's attempt to construct a suit of armour where investor claims of mismanagement are concerned. Investment firms are legally required to have new investors complete such a document as a guide to the investment strategy followed by the advisor in constructing a suitable portfolio. Investors are asked to estimate the degree of their investment knowledge, the level of acceptable risk they are prepared to endure, and the value of their liquidable assets, among other elements, as part of their account-opening activity.

How effective are KYC forms? "Really stupid," according to Meir Statman, professor of finance at the Leavey School of Business, Santa Clara University. "Unfortunately, investors think they must answer them. If you ask someone, 'How many stars do you think there are in the heavens?' they have no idea. But they'll probably still answer the question. Same with investment knowledge."

Statman went on to make a provocative and instantly comprehensible statement: "We all want two things in life. One is to be rich and the other is not to be poor. [For most people,] not being poor is more important than being rich ... On that basis, I think the primary responsibility of advisors is to protect the downside of their client's portfolio."*

---

*Mark Noble, *Building a Better Risk Profile*, Advisor.ca, March 10, 2009.

How Much Risk Can You Tolerate?

RRSP/RRIF/TFSA investments are directed toward providing post-employment income, but determining how much will be needed (beyond "As much as possible!") is complex. The objective of saving and investing during your working years could include generating inheritances to assist your children, pay college and university tuition for grandchildren, create a trust or bequest for favourite charities or causes, and a dozen other goals, each with its own priority and target value.

Another variable reflects market situations at the time the risk assessment is made. Ask an uninformed investor about his risk tolerance after a steady rise in the market index over several months and he is likely to claim it's relatively high. Why not? What's to risk? When the bulls vanish and the bears take over, his risk tolerance will decline in relation to the market's devaluation.

Filling in the data demanded by KYC forms and risk-assessment questionnaires is like drinking a cup of chicken broth when you're battling a bad cold; it makes you feel good but it doesn't address the basic problem. Nor can it do so automatically. No trustworthy mathematical formula exists that will crunch figures based on your age, income, knowledge level, assets, net worth, time horizon, and other information and then spit out your level of risk tolerance.

Some astute advisors disregard all of this feel-good formulation and ask prospective clients a question that can be answered with a simple yes or no: If I invested $100,000 of your money today, and 10 years from now handed you back $200,000, would you be satisfied?

In almost every instance, the answer is "Yes." This means the client would—or should—be content with an average 7 percent annual return on the initial investment, a level that historically can be achieved at least 75 percent of the time.

Is Your Risk Tolerance High or Low, Steady or Variable, Real or Imaginary?

To this point, the term *risk* has been used as though it has a near-universal definition. In truth, it hasn't. No one can determine or even estimate your definition of risk (as it relates to your investments) and the degree of risk you are willing to tolerate.

So here is a test with neither right nor wrong answers. The purpose of these questions is to persuade you to determine your own risk personality, then consider it when reading the rest of this book.

Write your responses to the following questions, then take a few moments to reflect on them when you have finished. You might consider marking this page and returning to it when you have completed this book, and perhaps a few weeks later, when you have absorbed changes in the value of your portfolio, either up or down.

1 You are on board a sinking ship heading toward port. The ship is taking on water even as it keeps steaming forward. At what point, measured in percentages (0% = full flotation, 100% = sunk beneath the waves), do you jump into the water and hope you swim safely to shore?

   ☐ 10%   ☐ 20%   ☐ 30%
   ☐ 50%   ☐ 70%   ☐ You won't jump

2 Of these events, rate the one you fear most with a value of 1, the next 2, and so on to 5, the one you fear least.

   Collapse in the value of your investment portfolio   ☐
   Loss of employment   ☐
   Alienation from family   ☐
   Serious illness or death of spouse   ☐
   Global war   ☐

3 Using the same rating system, which of these do you fear is most
   likely to occur over the next 10 years?
   Loss of your job   ☐
   Personal bankruptcy   ☐
   Destruction/loss of your home   ☐
   50% decline in value of your investment portfolio   ☐
   Serious illness or debilitating accident to you or spouse   ☐

4 Again, using the same system, rate these decisions in order of the
   greatest risk they represent to you:
   Crossing a busy street in the middle of the block   ☐
   Neglecting to have a flu shot each year   ☐
   Smoking   ☐
   Making investment decisions   ☐
   Avoiding exercise/ignoring weight gain   ☐

5 A commission-based advisor brings you an investment opportunity that is widely acknowledged as legitimate. The advisor, who
   will make 10 percent sales commission on the transaction, assures
   you that the investment will yield a minimum 20 percent net
   return for you over the next 12 months. How much of your
   portfolio would you agree to invest in it?
   10 % ☐   25% ☐   40% ☐   50% ☐
   75% ☐   All of it ☐   None of it ☐

The Surest Thing to Remember in Investing:
There Are No Sure Things

I keep an investment book in my library that is either laughable or
tragic, depending upon your point of view and experience. It's there
not because it makes me feel superior but because it serves the same
role as the slave whose duty it was to whisper in the ear of the Roman

emperor when the emperor was receiving accolades from the cheering populace, "You are not a god; you are a mere mortal." Or something like that (I wasn't there at the time).

The book is titled *The 50 Best Internet Stocks for Canadians, 2001 Edition.* Among the advice readers could glean from the book: Buy Quality ("Leaders in their sectors or upstarts with high growth potential"); Don't Worry about High Share Prices ("Share price does not matter"); Accumulate—Don't Buy and Sell; and Start Immediately ("The sooner you get started ... the greater your potential for long-term returns.")

Timing isn't everything; it's the only thing. The authors and publishers of *The 50 Best Internet Stocks for Canadians* (Mark Pavan, Gene Walden, and Tom Shaugnessy; Toronto: MacMillan Canada, 2000) had all the timing of a one-eyed drunk in a chorus line. On Friday, March 10, 2000, around the time their book was published, the tech-heavy NASDAQ Composite Index peaked at 5038. On Monday, March 13, it began dropping faster than a skydiving rhino, sinking almost 80 percent in value.

The authors' timing was not only bad, their recommendations were appalling. Of the 50 best internet stocks for Canadians to accumulate in 2001, guess which rated numero uno, the pick of the litter, the cream of the crop, the first past the post?

Nortel.

In September 2000, when Canadians were browsing through *The 50 Best Internet Stocks for Canadians,* seeking ways to profit from the mountain that was really a bubble, Nortel stock topped $200 per share, defying the NASDAQ collapse. Expensive? Cheap at the price, the authors concluded. It rated four stars (the highest rating) each for earnings progression, revenue growth, stock growth, and consistency. How many stars should we give the authors for accuracy? (In mid-2009, if you had a quarter in your pocket, you could acquire a share of Nortel.)

The authors were not the only people in Canada, or in the global investment industry for that matter, who failed to foresee the meltdown of Nortel and the entire tech bubble. Major damage to Canadian investment portfolios, especially those within the RRSPs of Canadians over 50, was inflicted by dealers, advisors, brokers, or anyone who had a certificate from the Canadian Securities Course on their wall or in their drawer, entitling them to deal in securities and assist clients to reach their financial goals. They assumed conservative financial-planning principles could be set aside during market boom years, and they ignored mandatory planning processes such as asking, "When do we take profits?" And they were wrong—dramatically, spectacularly wrong.

Let's Be Realistic

Examining the relationship between financial advisors and RRSP investors over the past decade or so, I have been struck by the lack of one element in particular: realism.

Investors too often are unrealistic about the prospects and degree of long-term growth for their portfolios. Beginning investors overestimate the amount of assistance they can expect if their portfolio is minuscule in size. A couple of thousand dollars may represent wealth to you, but if that's the value of your portfolio, don't expect a professional advisor to respond to your queries every time the market slips a few points.

Experienced investors fare no better when it comes to realistic expectations. It is not realistic for investors to expect near-continuous positive returns without losses and pullbacks. Yet some (supposedly) informed people in the marketplace never questioned claims made by Bernie Madoff in the United States, or homegrown fraudsters such as Michael Holoday here in Canada, that they could deliver consistently higher returns than the market with no risk of loss, even when the overall market declined. Would you believe someone who promised sunshine every day of the year in Canada? That's the scale of the promises made by Madoff, Holoday, and allegedly by Earl Jones.*

The events of 2008–2009 were not pleasant for anyone in the investment industry, clients and advisors alike. Investors grew first frantic then angry at the losses that appeared in their monthly statements, and aimed their anger at the people who, in many instances, had constructed their now-gutted portfolios. Was their anger justified? Not according to some advisors, who vented their rage at clients in industry forums with comments such as these:

Yes, the current market has taken everyone by surprise, but regardless of the KYC, people (will) still attack anyone … and try to blame someone else for the drop in their portfolios.

If people are going to invest, then they must be informed that there is risk. Nothing is guaranteed.

And my favourite, posted by an obviously irritated financial advisor:

I have been reliably informed that human beings have only three essential needs: food, shelter, and someone else to blame.

Cute. Perhaps someone should draw this advisor's attention to the fact that Canadians are attracted to the services of financial advisors by promises made through advertising and promotion on behalf of investment firms. Who is really to blame if investors respond to pitches such as the following, culled from various media and marketing vehicles in mid-2009?

---

*For more on them and others, and the techniques they employ, see Chapter 8: Wolves on the Road to Grandma's House.

Our advisors work ... to deliver customized investment solutions and integrated wealth plans that meet the diverse financial needs and goals of our clients.

—Assante

You can trust in our expertise to help build a wealth management strategy uniquely designed to achieve your wealth management objectives.

—BMO Nesbitt Burns

Do you want to go it alone? Or do you want to get expertise on your side, to help you devise an investment strategy that can work for you, no matter what you're investing for?

—CIBC Wood Gundy

A dedicated professional, your Investment Advisor devotes time to fully understand your financial situation, life goals and tolerance for risk when creating a strategy that is right for you ...

—RBC Dominion Securities

Your ScotiaMcLeod advisor's top priority is gaining a comprehensive understanding of your needs, so that he or she can develop a strategic plan to help you reach your goals.

—ScotiaMcLeod

You will receive comprehensive and personalized investment advice while staying involved in the key decisions about your portfolio.

—TD Waterhouse

We will provide a personal, thoughtful and intelligent strategy, delivered by a highly qualified professional you can trust.

—Wellington West

Banks and investment firms are hardly the first to stretch the truth in their promotional come-ons. The key point is that they are all promising to deliver the same thing: personalized service dedicated to individual investor needs and goals, along with heavy dollops of trust. So why doesn't this translate into better protection for client assets in the event of a market meltdown? Why should aggrieved investors be told "markets go down as well as up," and be expected to nod dutifully and go away?

Choosing an Advisor. It's a Little Like Choosing a Spouse ...

I'm not convinced that all Canadians need financial advisors to ride shotgun on their clients' retirement-savings vehicles, but I believe most do. That's because too few of us pay sufficient attention to the investments we're making to finance our future. We can't repair the transmission in our cars, but we know how to use and maintain them. Unfortunately, the same cannot be said for Canadians and their RRSPs.

The process of choosing a good financial advisor is a little like choosing a mate, in a couple of aspects (and not at all in others). Here are some guidelines:

- Chemistry is critical. If you do not feel that the advisor honestly relates to your investment needs and expectations, keep looking.

- Honesty is essential, on two levels. The first, of course, is based on trust. The other is based on the advisor's policy of expressing caution and disagreement with proposals from you if the proposals conflict with a strategy you have both agreed upon.

- Third-party involvement is essential. Many of the advisor horror stories you hear concern independent individuals who accept your funds, manage your portfolios, issue statements and cheques, and generally function as a one-man/woman show. Should you choose an advisor who is not associated with a large and prominent firm, do not grant him or her the right to make withdrawals or write cheques on your account, and insist that your portfolio is held by a third party who acts as an independent custodian and issues the monthly statements.

- One person alone cannot handle a number of client portfolios. Look for backup staff and support.

What should you realistically expect from an advisor? Three things:

1 **Transparency.** A good advisor explains why he or she is recommending a particular investment vehicle, how it matches your investment strategy, and how much it is costing you.

2 **Honesty.** Without dragging in the prurient aspect, your relationship with a financial or investment advisor should resemble the one you share with your spouse. Lying is betrayal, and betrayal is intolerable.

3 **Protection.** Beware of "Yes!" men (or women). Some of the most valued services a good advisor can provide extend beyond "You should …" to include "You shouldn't …"—especially if the negative comment is in response to an unsuitable investment idea you have. Good advice in any situation consists of offering differing opinions, discussing them with the client, suggesting intelligent action, and preventing unwise client actions.

7

FEES, COMMISSIONS, AND OTHER HOLES IN YOUR BUCKET

Various routes toward becoming a financial advisor can be pursued, but few resemble the one chosen by Preet Banerjee.

"I was originally interested in neuroscience," Banerjee recalls in his office overlooking Glen Abbey Golf Course in Oakville, Ontario. "I loved the analytical approach it involved. My father is a physician and I knew a neurosurgeon, so I had an opportunity to watch him at work a few times."

Halfway through his University of Toronto neuroscience studies, Banerjee realized he wanted to experience direct and immediate gratification for his life's work, whatever it might be. "And there is no immediate gratification from research," he comments. But there is in motor racing, his first stop after leaving university. "I enrolled at the Bridgestone Racing Academy," Banerjee says, "obtained my racing licence, and spent two years helping to manage the facility."

As manager, he met a Toronto-based investment banker who, impressed with the younger man's abilities, offered him a job. That's where Banerjee's fascination with analysis and need for quick response came together. Applying the same focused manner used in his medical studies and race car training, Banerjee successfully wrote five different examinations for his DMS (Derivatives Market

Specialist) designation within seven weeks after completing the
Canadian Securities Course, the Professional Financial Planning
Course, and studies in Wealth Management Techniques. He also
holds FMA (Financial Management Advisor) qualifications.

Now a senior vice-president with Pro-Financial Asset Management,
Banerjee is an outspoken critic of actively managed mutual funds
and the high fees and commissions associated with them, a point
he emphasizes on his appropriately titled website,
Wheredoesallmymoneygo.com.

"High fees are a reflection of what the market will bear," he
says without hesitation. "If people aren't saying with their wallets,
'No, we are sick of this,' [the fund companies] are going to keep
offering them because [the companies] are making lots of money."

The mutual fund companies also succeed thanks to the herd
mentality of both investors and mutual fund managers. Fund
managers may outperform the competition and become stars, but
they can do this only by avoiding the "groupthink" mentality of the
industry (remember: "When everybody thinks the same way,
nobody is thinking at all"). This, of course, injects risk into the
quotient, because if the manager fails to succeed and falls substantially behind the industry average, he or she is likely to be fired.

"There is very little incentive to say, 'Forget what everyone else
is doing, I'm going to be different'," Banerjee points out. If the fund
in question mirrors the appropriate index by 80 percent—and both
Banerjee and an analysis of individual fund holdings suggest they
do—why do investors pay MERs several times higher than those
charged on ETFs? And why, as we saw earlier, are the MERs
themselves the highest in all the countries studied by
Morningstar.com?

Banerjee, who has achieved more hard-to-obtain designations
beyond his degree in neuroscience and racing licence than the vast
majority of financial advisors and planners, notes two other factors:
the minimum requirements for entry into the profession, and a

remuneration system that emphasizes brokerage profits over investor earnings.

"The educational requirements are far too low," Banerjee suggests. "Think of the undergraduate studies, internships, residencies, and so on that a physician requires, or the articling experience of a lawyer, and post-graduate studies needed for teachers, engineers and other professions." He shakes his head. "Yet somebody who takes a couple of weeks to study and pass an exam based on data off the internet can be put in charge of somebody's life savings. That's wrong."

You may be aware that the vast majority of broker-employed advisors are paid according to the commissions they earn for their employer. You may not know that high-volume producers not only earn more commissions, but earn a greater proportion of the commissions they bring in. Note how the proportion climbs with productivity on this typical remuneration grid:

GROSS COMMISSION	TRANSACTION EARNINGS AND PAYOUT LEVELS				
	$0–$100	$100–$200	$200–$300	$400–$500	$500+
$0–$100K/year	10%	20%	20%	20%	20%
$100K–$200k/year	25%	25%	25%	25%	47%
$300k–$400k/year	35%	39%	43%	44%	49%
$400k–$500k/year	40%	42%	44%	46%	51%
$500k–$1M/year	42%	44%	46%	48%	53%
$1M–$2M/year	44%	46%	48%	50%	55%
$2M+/year	49%	51%	53%	55%	57%

SOURCE: Wheredoesallmymoneygo.com.

A broker or advisor earning less than $100,000 annually might persuade a client to invest $5000 in a mutual fund with a 5 percent commission. Of the $250 generated for the firm ($5000 × 5 percent), the advisor receives 20 percent of the earnings, a mere $50. Should the same advisor earn from $400,000 to $500,000 in annual commissions, he or she now keeps 44 percent of $250, or $110.

A production incentive? Sure. But this is not about an appliance salesperson being encouraged to sell more microwave ovens; it concerns the handling of lifetime savings to generate a retirement income for individuals often unfamiliar with the products and services selected for them. Most Canadians know far more about the features and operation of microwaves than they will ever know about the design, structure, management, performance, and relative suitability of mutual funds, bonds, and other investment vehicles. They seek guidance and assistance from individuals who claim to be dedicated to maximizing the clients' assets while encouraged to boost their commission earnings to ever-higher levels.

This is not a production incentive; it is a behaviour modifier. High-volume producers are rewarded with dramatically higher earnings. Low-volume people are motivated either to generate more commissions or leave the business.

Imagine this scenario: Employed as a financial advisor by a firm using the accompanying commission remuneration grid, you find yourself on December 20 with $398,000 in earned commissions for the year. If you can earn another $2000 in commission by year's end, you'll move into a new remuneration level, providing a larger portion of all the commissions earned since January. The portion of earned commissions flowing into your pocket will increase by 5 percent. With $400,000 in earnings for the year, you'll earn $160,000 instead of $140,000, a fat $20,000 return for scoring a mere $2000 in gross commissions. Would you be tempted to find clients who would respond to transactions generating $2000, whether or not they were ideally suitable for the clients' needs? Of course you would. The system doesn't mean big producers receive more pieces of the pie; it means each piece they receive grows bigger in size.

"Ah," you may say, "just because someone *can* earn more money so easily does not mean that he or she *will* do it." Or so you wish. The investment industry may not have more devils within it than other professions. But there is no evidence that it has more angels either.

"Churning"—It's about Making Money, Not Making Butter

If your remuneration is based on the number of transactions you conduct, and the incentive links the size of the earned commissions to the amount you earn in direct proportion, you look for ways to generate more transactions. The most productive method is to maximize the number of transactions in client accounts, with or without the clients' permission, a practice called *churning*.

This, you will not be surprised to learn, is frowned upon by people who set the rules in the investment industry. The practice continues, however, at a greater rate than the industry knows or acknowledges. In fact, in a landmark study conducted on behalf of the Ontario Securities Commission by a former OSC commissioner, the practice of paying trailer fees to advisors, brokers, and mutual fund salespeople was reluctantly defended because the fees tended to reduce the temptation of these people to engage in churning as a means of enhancing their incomes.*

---

*Glorianne Stromberg, *Regulatory Strategies for the Mid 90s: Recommendations for Regulating Investment Funds in Canada*, p. 59: "Part of my reluctance simply to recommend that trailer or service fees be banned relates to the concern expressed by industry participants that banning these fees would just encourage sales representatives to increase the transactions within their clients' accounts or to abandon their clients after the initial sale. There is concern that even with enhancing the supervisory controls and procedures, it is unrealistic to think that the measures will be sufficient to prevent switching and churning of accounts."

Trailer fees are commissions paid annually to financial advisors by mutual fund companies whose units the advisors have sold to their clients. The fees, typically 0.5 percent of the value of the held units at the end of each year, represent either a means of remunerating advisors for guidance, a reward for persuading clients to retain the units despite the fund's performance, or an industry-approved method of preventing churning.

The investment industry prefers the first definition because advisors shouldn't be expected to work for nothing. Fine. But should they also get paid for *doing* nothing? And should investors pay a premium to encourage their advisor to stick to the straight and narrow instead of engaging in illegal practices?

An advisor earning trailer fees of 0.5 percent on a $500,000 portfolio receives a cheque from the grateful mutual fund each year of $2500 in return, we are told, for being a good little boy or girl. Many advisors in Canada can boast $10 million, $20 million, and more in client assets managed within the advisor's book. Every million dollars in qualifying mutual funds feeds $5000 a year to the brokerage or advisor, year after year. Forgetting the argument that trailer fees discourage churning, is the advisor's counsel worth it? Perhaps. But only if it's provided. And there is damn little evidence this is the case.

Remember Trimark, the mutual fund company that set a standard for performance and general excellence in the 1980s and 1990s? When founders Robert Krembil and Arthur Labatt realized the enormous growth of Trimark meant their policy of limiting the fund's portfolio to 40 companies was no longer viable, they sold the firm to American giant Invesco.

Invesco bought two things: Income from the billions of dollars held in Trimark funds by Canadians attracted by its past performance, and the Trimark brand, added to Invesco's long list of other mutual funds. Almost nothing else of the Krembil–Labatt formula remained. Invesco brags that it manages $350 billion in investor funds. Trimark represents

$5 billion, or 1.5 percent of Invesco's total assets under management. If you believe Invesco will consider restoring a formula for exceptional performance as successful in the future as Trimark's was in the past, perhaps you will also believe the sun will rise in the west tomorrow morning. The majority of Trimark fund managers who absorbed Krembil's wisdom during the years he directed the firm bailed out when Trimark's new Houston-based owners strode through the front door.

Virtually everybody in the Canadian investment business world knew of the Invesco takeover of Trimark, and of the exodus from the fund of management and support staff dating back to its glory days. The massive management change had a negative effect on the fund's already shoddy performance.

If you were a Trimark investor not plugged into the investment industry scuttlebutt, you would have known nothing about the change unless your advisor alerted you to the situation. Fat chance. Between November 2007 and February 2009, Canadians who were invested in Trimark funds watched the value of their portfolios sink like large stones in deep waters, unaware of the wholesale management upheaval behind it. The Trimark Fund lost half its value in that period, its losses consistently exceeding other funds in their group. Most Trimark investors who complained about the poor performance were reassured by advisors to maintain their position. Other investors played detective and discovered the reason on their own.

"By the time I found out what was going on," one Trimark unit holder muttered, "I lost about one-third of my money. Neither Trimark nor [RBC] Dominion Securities bothered to alert me. I complained to Trimark CEO Peter Intraligi and the regional manager of Dominion Securities. I said they were both professionally negligent in not looking out for my interests."*

---

*Posted on www.cbc.ca, April 12, 2009.

Trimark's response was to state they were not obligated to alert unit holders of management changes; the brokerage claimed they did not make the change known because they believed the funds were "in good shape."

If the unit holders had purchased shares of a publicly traded company, the firm would have been obligated to alert them of takeovers and management changes. Investing in the fund holding the shares instead of the shares themselves negated this obligation. The investors were on their own with the brokerages and advisors, many suspected, because the commission-based industry folk didn't want to disturb those annual Trimark trailer fees.

Once again: Trailer fees are defended as a means of avoiding churning by "unethical" advisors. So what do you call advisors who sit around waiting for the annual trailer fee cheques to arrive instead of alerting clients to changes that could deflate their portfolios?

The reality is this: Trailer fees are unnecessary to prevent churning, which is relatively easy to track by observing transaction records. Here, for example, is the record of 166 "switches" or transactions recorded in 22 client accounts over two months by Leo Alexander O'Brien, a mutual fund salesman employed by a firm in St. John's, Newfoundland and Labrador:

DATES	CLIENT(S)	SWITCHES	TOTAL	FEES
April 20/05–June 16/06	PF and PF	6	$136,185.69	$2723.71
April 20/05–June 16/06	CS	9	$126,680.26	$2763.80
Apr. 22/05–June 16/06	CS	7	$164,039.03	$1623.82
Apr. 21/05–June 16/06	GP	6	$216,512.16	$3199.17
Apr. 20/05–June 16/06	MP	6	$193,332.37	$4059.55
July 29/05–June 16/06	MP	5	$53,064.40	$1061.29
Apr. 26/05–June 16/06	PP	14	$714,115.33	$11,904.86

Apr. 22/05–June 16/06	PH and DH	6	$140,644.26	$925.78
Apr. 22/05–June 16/06	DA	6	$139,604.64	$913.21
Apr. 21/05–June 16/06	ES and IS	6	$128,292.84	$2565.86
Apr. 22/05–June 19/06	JL	6	$169,300.64	$2188.87
Apr. 20/05–June 15/06	JL	9	$517,524.05	$8121.68
Apr. 21/05–June 16/06	RE	6	$268,854.87	$5377.10
Apr. 20/05–June 16/06	JWH	6	$114,423.51	$2288.57
Apr. 20/05–June 16/06	JH	12	$107,419.32	$2090.30
Apr. 20/05–June 16/06	FEB	7	$120,493.18	$2701.10
Apr. 20/05–June 16/06	FEB	10	$207,831.98	$3539.31
Apr. 21/05–June 16/05	MC	7	$58,814.70	$959.74
Apr. 21/05–June 16/06	LM	7	$45,430.14	$770.01
Apr. 20/05–June 16/06	NHN	8	$49,404.18	$835.68
Apr. 20/05–June 16/06	SEP	10	$149,815.05	$2326.46
Apr. 20/05–June 16/06	WP	7	$71,677.89	$1239.61
				Total $64,179.48

SOURCE: *The Mutual Fund Observer*, April 2, 2009.

In his defence, O'Brien claimed he was attempting to time the market and thus, it is presumed, generate greater returns on behalf of his clients. In fact, the only greater returns were recorded by O'Brien—more than $64,000 in fees—using Limited Trading Authorizations (LTAs), agreements with clients that permitted him to conduct trades without their direction. Before joining the firm where this churning took place, O'Brien had been dismissed from a number of other dealers for similar activity. O'Brien's branch manager was aware of his blemished record and watched the trades pile up, yet failed to stop the practice, which cost both him and O'Brien their careers in the investment industry.

Let's remember that RRSP transactions aren't conducted by a bunch of guys wearing aprons shouting across a trading pit. They're conducted by computers, and any nerd who can tell an Intel chip from a tortilla chip can design a program that will alert a brokerage compliance officer to excessive trading, assuming the brokerage wants to know. To date, the industry refuses to install such a system. And how much has this cost investors?

"We Lost Your Money. Now You Owe Us More."

Some investment firms find ways to charge new fees based on errors they make that cost their clients money. One investor, responding to a CBC-TV story criticizing the investment industry, reported that an advisor insisted on moving all of her husband's $85,000 RRSP assets into technology-based funds just prior to the collapse of that sector in 2000. Her husband questioned the wisdom of the move, but responding to the advisor's supposedly wider knowledge and strong persuasion, he acquiesced. The resulting crash reduced the couple's retirement fund to about $12,000, a heartbreaking disaster. Then, because the account value had fallen below the brokerage's minimum threshold of $15,000, the brokerage slapped an annual management fee on the account.* Still wonder who really gets rich from the investment industry?

Abuses of the commission system, and calls for its abolition or substantial revision, have generated much discussion since I raised the issue in my book *The Naked Investor*. A fee-based system, while not perfect, strikes most people as a worthy improvement. Progress is being made, at glacial speed. Some mutual fund companies now offer F-Class funds, which typically reduce their MER by 1 percent, pay no commissions, and enable fee-based advisors to charge a direct 1-percent annual fee. The move was inspired by a groundswell of demand from investor advocates, who began asking, "Instead of paying these professionals as

---

*Posted on www.cbc.ca, April 12, 2009.

though they are selling used cars, why not pay them the same way other professionals are paid, with fees or salaries?"

Why not indeed? Many independent advisors operate in this manner with great success, although fee-based advisors need a substantial number of fair-sized client portfolios to generate incomes comparable with their commission-based compatriots. An independent advisor with 100 accounts averaging $300,000 in assets may do well by charging a flat 1 percent annual fee, but a similar arrangement for an advisor with 50 accounts averaging $50,000 in assets is not going to hold much appeal. According to many in the investment industry, the large bank-owned brokerages are not likely to support a move to fees; they are more likely to move to a salary-based system of compensation, an unpopular move for advisors but perhaps a step forward for investors.

Advisors, brokers, and mutual fund salespeople are not salary-prone for the most part. While not every investment firm in the country abides by an "Eat what you kill" philosophy, the industry attracts competitive spirits who, for the most part, prefer a linkage between their success and their compensation levels even if it means forgoing a steady income.

Until 1996, Canadians could deduct fees paid to advisors managing their RRSPs and RRIFs from taxable income, a substantial aid to enhancing growth within these plans and promoting the concept of fee-based investing. (The fees remain tax-deductible for non-registered investments.) A little long-distance perception—a rare and nocturnal beast in the halls of government, to be sure—would have recognized that enhancing the growth of RRSPs would return dividends to the country's tax coffers, since every dollar withdrawn from an RRSP or RRIF is subject to tax.

Moving from a commission-based system to a fee-based method of remuneration would not eliminate all the problems investors have with the industry. But with a few basic ground rules in place it would contribute to transparency and reduce the temptation to churn accounts. If the mavens who call the shots in Ottawa dealt with the same pension investment concerns as the rest of us, they would likely spot this benefit and act accordingly. As we saw, their interest in the pension concerns of Canadians in the private sector appears as low as a Saskatoon thermometer's reading on a January night. Tax-deductible RRSP fees? As my cynical mother might have advised, "Don't hang by your thumbs waiting, kid."

The Long-Term Importance of Small Differences

No matter how well your investments may be performing, saving 1 percent in annual costs is as rewarding as earning an extra percentage from the performance of your investments.

Consider four investors: Mary, at 30 years of age; Marvin, at 40 years of age; Mattie, at 50 years of age; and Mike at 60 years of age. All expect to retire at age 70 and are counting on the performance of their RRSP to generate the money they'll need.

Mary, who has been contributing to her plan for 10 years, has accrued $50,000 in her RRSP. Marvin has $100,000, Mattie has $200,000, and Mike is sitting on $400,000. (I like to keep things simple for the sake of making one point crystal clear.)

Assume each averages 7 percent annual return over the years between now and their retirement date. Now assume that, because of high fees, excessive commissions, and the usual leaks in their investment bucket, they lose a mere 1 percent annually, reducing their average yield to 6 percent. Would they miss it? Would you?

	AGE	YEARS TO GO	CURRENT VALUE	AT RETIREMENT 6%	7%	DIFFERENCE
Mary	30	40	$50,000	$514,285	$748,723	+$234,438
Marvin	40	30	$100,000	$574,350	$761,225	+$186,875
Mattie	50	20	$200,000	$641,427	$773,937	+$132,510
Mike	60	10	$400,000	$716,339	$786,860	+$70,521

The enormous difference of nearly a quarter-million dollars in Mary's balance—remember, this assumes no further contributions to their RRSPs—illustrates the magic of compound interest. More to the point, all four examples show the importance of reducing drain, even in relatively small portions, from an investment. The loss of 10, 20, 30 percent or more of the value of your equities as a result of a drop in stock market values is heart-stopping to be sure. But markets, as we must keep reminding ourselves, bounce back. Losses due to high commissions, taken in dribbles of even 1 percent a year, are gone for good.

Three Unfair but True Observations about Financial Advisors

Why "unfair"? Because most financial advisors are honest people who enjoy their work and care for their clients' assets. Too many, regrettably, invest more time and effort lining their own pockets than nurturing the nest eggs of the people who depend on them. In this business the bad guys (and gals) don't wear black hats; you won't know which side of the line they're working until it's too late. So keep these facts in mind:

1 **Financial advisors and brokers are salespeople.** They earn their living by selling things. If they don't sell, they don't eat. Some of them are very careful that whatever they sell is suitable for the customer/client they are dealing with and make their decision on that basis. Others make their decision exclusively on the size of the commission they will earn. And they earn it from your money—no one else's.

2 **Education does not mean precise market knowledge.** Many advisors have more letters after their name than a can of alphabet soup. (I knew one mutual fund salesman who listed CSP among the designations on his business card. "I recognize the other initials," I said, "but I don't know what CSP stands for." "Canadian Ski Patrol," he smirked, "and you're the first person to ask me that.") Investing is an art, not

a science. Letters after their name mean the advisors have passed a series of examinations, not that they are flawless in plotting strategies and identifying investment opportunities.

3 **Education does not ensure ethics.** Credentials and certification provide the owner with the right to proffer advice and deal in securities. They do not provide you with assurance that everything the advisor does will be in your interest and to your benefit exclusively.

8

WOLVES ON THE ROAD TO GRANDMA'S HOUSE

"They set the tempo the minute they meet you," former Toronto Metro Police fraud squad investigator Gary Logan comments. "After they get to know you well enough, they determine how they can use your confidence in them to victimize you."

He's talking about fraudsters, especially those who prey on middle-aged and older RRSP and RRIF owners. Over his 17 years of investigating, charging, and helping convict fraud artists, Logan has encountered every scheme and every tactic imaginable.

Logan's point about criminals setting the tempo explains much of their success when dealing with cautious individuals who cannot believe they are in danger of being swindled—until they are.

"The most successful of the criminals posing as financial advisors," Logan explains in his suburban Toronto office, "see their clients as opportunities. They have a knack of building confidence in their victims. They'll make any promise necessary to get the other person's money into their own pocket. Afterwards, they'll deliver promises to retain the victim's confidence, keep them happy, and delay the day when it all falls apart."

Logan is employed with Garda Security, applying his experience earned from tracking frauds and their perpetrators to Garda clients concerned about recovering lost funds. He focuses on assembling material for civil actions instead of criminal courts, but his outrage at the antics of fraudsters has not abated. He has seen too many Canadians lose their life savings to people with too much greed and no conscience, and is intent on offering whatever advice he can that might reduce the number of victims.

His first suggestion sounds like a parental directive: "Do your homework."

Before discussing an investment opportunity with anyone, Logan suggests, understand what is being proposed and how it works. Rely on another trusted source for information, not the one who is offering you the deal. "Go into it with your eyes wide open," Logan says, "understanding the costs and the risks. Do not go into any investment opportunity with the idea of getting an education on the topic," he emphasizes, "because the first lesson you'll get is whatever the other person wants you to know."

Making an investment decision immediately is also unwise. "If you have to act now," Logan advises, "don't." You've spent years building your savings or portfolio; why take minutes to decide to pass it along to someone else?

His closing observation brings to mind the thousands of wealthy and intelligent people scammed out of billions of dollars by invest-ment guru Bernie Madoff. "Once you've made some sort of commitment to them," Logan says, "after you've shaken their hand and agreed to the deal, you'll buy into almost anything the fraud-sters will say or promise."

"How could intelligent people fall for such obvious scams?" we may ask ourselves when reading about various investment frauds. Because they made a commitment built on trust, and that changes everything.

In early 2009, the biggest name in investment fraud was Bernie Madoff. He earned it. While the exact amount of investors' money lost by Madoff may never be known, the figure appears to be in the neighbourhood of $50 billion, which is a very wealthy neighbourhood indeed.

More impressive even than the cost of Madoff's shenanigans was the list of people he bamboozled. These weren't folks like you and me, hoping to squirrel enough in our retirement accounts to cover an annual trudge on a sandy beach each winter. Madoff's victims included the immensely wealthy, the impressively astute, and the witheringly skeptical.

The lesson to be learned is clear: If these people can be defrauded so completely, anyone is vulnerable to similar actions by similar miscreants. And while Bernie Madoff operated in the United States, preying upon generally wealthy individuals, antics like his occur frequently on this side of the border.

A study conducted in 2007* revealed that about 20 percent of Canadians had been offered an apparent fraudulent investment in the previous three years. Of these, fewer than one out of five bothered to report it to the authorities. Why? Because, most replied, they believed the offer was so blatantly fraudulent that no rational person would invest in it.

Ah, but they do. Nearly 5 percent of Canadians have been victims of investment fraud at some point in their lives. That's more than a million of us who have fallen for a pitch that separates us from our money as efficiently as a carnival barker or a racetrack tout, and three out of four victims failed to recover any of the money handed over.

The extent of investment fraud in Canada could be even wider than the study suggests, because only a minority of victims actually report the incident to police. Perhaps they're embarrassed at their own gullibility, or they believe fraud artists find a way to beat the justice system. On the latter point, they may be correct. About 70 percent of Canadians are

---

*Canadian Securities Administrators/Investor Education Committee, *2007 CSA Investor Study: Understanding the Social Impact of Investment Fraud*, Innovative Research Group, Inc.

convinced that fraudsters either avoid conviction or, if actually tried and found guilty, receive sentences so light they're almost a joke.

There Are Frauds and Scams. And Then There Are *FREE SEMINARS!*

Building a prospect list is hard work if you're a broker or financial advisor. You can spend years assisting clients to structure their portfolios, trusting them to tell friends and family how pleased they are with your service and hoping you harvest business from their referrals.

You can always make cold calls, which involves spending hours with a telephone directory, calling people at random and being humiliated by a hundred hang-ups, with the faint hope of netting a single new client.

Or you can host a free investment seminar. All you need is a hall, a coffee maker, and an investment celebrity whose name and smiling face will attract a crowd.

The investment celebrity breed has shrunk somewhat since I dedicated an entire chapter to it in the original edition of *The Naked Investor*. Five years ago, Brian Costello, Garth Turner, and Jerry White were as unavoidable in the media around RRSP time as bank and mutual fund advertisements. Since then, Costello has been legally banned from the securities industry, Turner had another brief spin in Ottawa political circles and now spends his time cranking out books predicting a financial apocalypse, and the last I heard of White was a scheduled appearance at the Legion Hall in Melville, Saskatchewan.

In their place are local celebrities—the term *shills* is more accurate—with radio call-in shows or newspaper columns to dispense their opinions on investing. They form a tag team with unscrupulous advisors and brokers, both of them feeding fears of inadequate growth in RRSP investments. The appeal looks reasonable and even entertaining: A popular investment guru will appear at a seminar to teach you, without cost or obligation, how to maximize the return on your retirement investments.* Hey, it's a night out with your spouse, right? Munch on a few snacks, sip some coffee or wine, and come home with your head full of great new investment ideas. Alas, you are likely to return with a mild sense of panic and a badly reconstructed investment portfolio.

The attack is usually two-pronged. First, the famous investment guru warns that most Canadians are ill-prepared to cope with retirement. Their RRSP contributions and balance are too low, their investments perform poorly, and their financial future is bleak. Without additional money and a more aggressive investment plan, the guru lectures, their retirement years may consist of eating cat food and sleeping alongside hot-air vents. Earning 7 or 8 percent annually on their RRSP investments is ludicrous. The rich don't settle for that—why should you? Homeowners in the audience are reminded that they occupy an asset that's doing nothing for them, referring to the $100,000, $200,000 or more in paid-up equity in their home. Why not put that equity to work by borrowing money against it, buying some high-yield investments, and writing off the interest payments against their income tax?

After the guru plants the bomb (and is paid several thousand dollars for his appearance), the brokers and advisors light the fuse. Armed with promotions and video presentations, the commissioned salespeople begin promoting whatever happens to be on the menu that day (some of these seminars are underwritten by mutual fund companies) as the means of achieving the guru's promises. The seminar sponsor may even arrange to have a mortgage lender on the site, prepared to set up loans secured by homeowners' equity. Many people who attend the seminars, believing them to be educational events and not the blatant marketing sessions they are, go home with the equity in their homes tied up in expensive and risky investments.

---

*For the record, I never have and never will participate in events of this kind.

I detailed these shady events in the first edition of *The Naked Investor,* and a well-known investment writer explained the appeal and profit of these seminars to advisors:

> If the advisor gets a hundred people to attend, and just 10 go along with the idea (of using home equity to finance an investment), each borrowing $100,000 to invest, that's $1 million in mutual fund sales or $50,000 in commissions for the advisor. Not bad for a night's work.*

This isn't outright fraud and, given the recent volatility in house prices and the market generally, the seminars aren't nearly as popular as they were five years ago. But the leveraged purchase of inappropriate investments in both registered and unregistered portfolios has led to disaster for thousands of Canadians.

By all means, educate yourself on basic investment skills and strategies, but do it from books such as this one that provide you with facts and permit you all the time you need to ponder your actions—not from "free" seminars sponsored by commission-based advisors whose pitch is set up by media celebrities.

Just When You Think You're Older and Wiser, You're Also Most Vulnerable to Fraud

Anyone with pocket change is a potential target for a fraud artist, but RRSP and LIRA investors age 50 and older represent prime prospects. The reason? More money and more trust.

At that age and beyond, many Canadians are balancing costs for dependent children at home or in university while perhaps supporting an aging parent or two. Meanwhile, retirement looms just a few birthdays

---

*The Naked Investor: Why Almost Everybody But You Gets Rich on Your RRSP (Toronto: Penguin, 2005), p. 146.

away. They may be at their maximum earning power, but they are also facing multiple demands on every dollar they make. And while they deal directly with the needs of both children and parents in a hands-on manner, they need help with their own retirement planning. Many are preparing themselves for Grandma's house, a cozy little place in the woods where the grandchildren come to visit with picnic baskets in hand. That's a lovely image. It's the wolves that spoil it.

The wolves do not sport hairy faces, oversized teeth, and pointed ears. They tend to wear expensive clothes and warm smiles, like honest and competent business people of all stripes, so wearing a cloak of suspicion alone won't keep you from becoming a victim.

Like the bedtime story of the wolf in Grandma's bed, many of the schemes employed by investment fraudsters have their roots in a fairy tale. Once upon a time, someone somewhere heard about an exceptional investment offer, took advantage of it, multiplied their money 5, 10, 20, or maybe 100 times, and lived happily ever after.

For every person who actually succeeded at doing this, hundreds of thousands of others, trying to replicate earlier success, have lost everything. If you like these odds, skip the next few pages. If you'd prefer to deal with the real world, keep reading.

Let's begin by identifying various types of investment fraud you could encounter.

Precious metals and gems. Diamonds, rubies, sapphires, and good old-fashioned gold may be offered at a price far below market value. Unless you're a gemologist or gold dealer, walk away. The gems will be glass and the gold will be almost anything but.

Ponzi schemes. This won't be labelled as such. In fact, you won't be able to identify one until you find yourself in fiscal communion with the victims of Bernie Madoff, who appears to have orchestrated history's largest Ponzi caper. (The trick's title is derived from the name of its first practitioner, Charles Ponzi, who bilked investors of $10 million back in the 1920s.) A Ponzi scheme consists of promising exceptional returns to early investors, paid with new money that pours in when others hear about the supposed earnings. It can be maintained only as long as new victims keep adding money to the pot, and eventually collapses.

Oil and gas producers. You wouldn't believe someone who claims to own land with large deposits of oil on it, and needs seed money to buy drilling equipment, would you? Thousands do every year, later discovering that neither the oil, the equipment, nor the land exists.

Foreign currency exchange (FOREX). Now, this one you can understand, you think. Your investment in Canadian money is used to purchase foreign currency at an exceptionally low rate of exchange. When the value of the foreign currency rises, it's converted back to loonies for a profit. Best of all, it's about real money. Or is it? The risk in dealing on the FOREX market is substantial, but don't worry about fluctuating exchange rates affecting your investment. Chances are your money will disappear into the coffers of the promoter and never be seen again. Not by you, at least.

Cattle, mink, fish, and beans. Or any similar commodity. The come-on may be based on a promise to buy the creatures or food at harvest time, with a large profit for you. The only harvest will occur, regardless of contracts or agreements, when you hand over your money.

Clever tax shelters. Fraudsters persuade RRSP owners to withdraw their assets as one lump sum of cash, pay the applicable tax, and invest the balance in products, industries, or locations (have you visited the

Cayman Islands recently?) where massive tax-free returns will quickly earn back the Canadian income tax. The products and industries may in fact be real, as will profits and commissions to the purveyors, but the tax-free status and the potential growth is illusory.

Special risk-free RRSP/LIRA loan. A variation on the above, this works when a promoter convinces you to invest all or most of your RRSP or LIRA in a new start-up company. It's a sweet deal: You purchase shares in the company, keep them within your RRSP or LIRA, and the promoter loans you back 50 percent or more of the shares' value in return for your support. That's as much as you might keep after tax if you had withdrawn the entire amount as cash. Now, you have both the shares and the cash, tax-free. That's the dream. Here's the reality: The shares, if you receive them, are worthless; the cash loan will never appear; and the Canada Revenue Agency (CRA) will spot the scam and come calling, demanding you pay tax on the cash loan you never received.

These schemes are not rare, nor are the victims who fall for them. In March 2009, the CRA reported it had reassessed more than 5000 Canadians who had participated in these deals, resulting in additional taxable income of $250 million.*

Double dipping. This one is especially bitter because it works on people who have already been scammed. The fraudster who stung you in the past sells your name to other crooks who contact you with a deal: They know who defrauded you, the scoundrels! They'll mention details only you and the original fraudster would know about to convince you of their credibility. Then they'll offer to help you recover most or all of your loss. For a fee, up front, of course.

---

*James Langton, "CRA Issues Warning on Tax-Free Withdrawal Schemes," *Investment Executive*, March 17, 2009.

Can you spot the danger here? Thousands of other didn't and sent money to these phoney Robin Hoods, losing even more of their money and pride.

✓ **Pump and dump.** You hear about a company whose stock is priced far lower than its actual value. If you act now and buy before the price rises, you'll make a major score. The stock is real—you can track the price on an exchange—and the price may rise, but that's only because others are falling for the same pitch. The person promoting the deal is holding a massive amount of stock. When the price gets high enough, the stock is dumped at a profit for the promoter, depressing the value to its true market level, which is substantially lower than the price you paid.

Affinity Fraud: Do You Know Who Your Friends Are?

In the late 1990s, about 300 members of a Seventh-Day Adventist church in Abbotsford, B.C., invested more than $11 million in a pooled fund investing in offshore companies. Joyfully declaring that he was an ex-pastor committing his life to spreading the munificence of the Lord among His believers, an American named Gary Stanhiser offered first the elders and later members of the congregation a blessed investment opportunity. Thanks to tax advantages between the B.C.–based pool and the foreign locations, Stanhiser explained, the profits promised to be immense. It was also, of course, quite legal, a concern for the devout churchgoers.

In fact, it was neither. None of the money was seen again, and for a number of years, hospitals in the Fraser Valley reported an inordinate number of cases of severe mental depression and stress-related injuries.*

Losing money you worked hard to acquire over years of effort is depressing on its own. Losing it to someone whose company you

---

*Patrick White, "Meet God's Fraud Squad," *The Globe and Mail*, October 4, 2007.

enjoyed and whose honesty you trusted can be devastating. Yet that's how most fraudsters succeed—by exploiting the trust they have created among family, friends, and club members.* As a mark of the total absence of honour among these lowlifes, incidents of affinity fraud occur among religious groups following sermons declaring the need for love and respect among the members.

Many people find affinity fraud the most difficult crime to avoid for the very reason it succeeds. Your guard would be aroused by a telephone call pitching a once-in-a-lifetime opportunity or offers muttered out of the side of their mouths by shady characters on a dark street. But Brother Smith who passes the collection plate each Sunday? Or George at the lodge hall? Or your daughter's brother-in-law? Surely they wouldn't be involved in something illegal and exploitive, would they?

Sadly, they may. The incidence of affinity fraud in Canada grows year by year, especially among minority groups and new immigrants, often isolated from mainstream society. This separation, along with language difficulties, makes it difficult for the members to access information, guidelines, and warnings. In a foreign environment, they place their trust in familiar names and cultural practices.

It's not necessary to suspect everyone with whom you have contact in your club, church, temple, synagogue, or gym. It's wise, however, to raise your defences whenever any of the following occur:

- New arrivals to an organization pitch investment deals to prominent members of the club, gaining influential support.

- The pitch includes schemes such as offshore banking, unique ways of playing the stock market, or investments in precious stones or metals.

- Not everyone is offered the opportunity to take advantage of this method of getting rich.

---

*For a detailed recounting of a classic case of affinity fraud, read my book *Free Rider: How a Bay Street Whiz Kid Stole and Spent $20 Million* (Toronto: MacArthur & Co., 2001).

- The promised returns are spectacular and the risk negligible.

- Requests for an explanation of the mechanics of the investment are met with scorn or confusing jargon.

Arm yourself against fraud with these attitudes and practices:

- Avoid being influenced by first impressions; con artists work hard to make a positive and memorable one.

- Never assume that anyone who holds the same religious beliefs as you must be as honourable as you.

- If someone pitches you an investment idea, ask, "What is the nature of the investment?" "Who receives my money?" "How will the money be used?" "What kind of security is provided for my money?" "How and when can I cash in my investment?" "Is there a prospectus?"

- Make a point of writing down answers, if any are provided.

- Do not permit yourself to be intimidated if the person making the pitch resents your questions, and don't be sidelined by smooth responses that flatter you while conveying few facts.

- Do not make any decision exclusively on the basis of an invest-ment closely tied to your faith, religious practices, club affiliation, or other association.

- Question the motive of any new member who quickly begins discussing investment or financial deals.

- It is not true that investments conducted within religious or fraternal organizations are not subject to regulations such as issuing a prospectus and licensing securities dealers; avoid anyone who disputes this fact.

- Check with your provincial securities commission to confirm that the individual promoting the investment opportunity is licensed.

- Do not allow yourself to be pressured into making an investment decision; if told you must decide immediately, walk away.

- Be skeptical of anyone who discourages you from obtaining advice from a lawyer, accountant, financial advisor, banker, or other professional.

- Never sign a document without reading it carefully; if any doubt or question persists, discuss its implications with a lawyer.

Here's one of the most maddening aspects of affinity fraud: *The perpetrators often get away with it.* In many cases, victims refuse to believe that someone so genial could possibly be crooked, and they avoid pursuing the matter until long after their money has vanished. Others are so embarrassed they prefer not to contact law enforcement, and chalk up their losses to experience. Meanwhile, the fraudsters have pocketed (or usually spent) the money, and are moving on to a new group of victims.

Gary Stanhiser, who is alleged to have masterminded the $11 million theft from the Fraser Valley Seventh-Day Adventist congregation, returned to his native California where he cheerily ignored the penalties of a $100,000 fine and a lifetime ban from working in the B.C. securities industry. No criminal charges were pursued.

9

Death and Taxes May Be Inevitable, but Substantial RRSP/RRIF Losses Are Not

Entering their 50s, Howard and Penny Mark* were looking forward to several years of comfort and relaxation. The Regina couple's children had completed their education and were pursuing their own lives, and the Marks anticipated playing the role of empty nesters. Then, two disasters struck.

The first was Howard's involvement in a serious auto accident. A drunk driver struck his car as he was returning from work one evening, leaving Howard permanently disabled. Through a combination of savings and support from Howard's employer, the couple had enough retirement savings to generate an adequate income. Within a year, the Marks agreed on a settlement with the other driver's insurance company that netted them about $650,000.

"We didn't want to take any chances," Penny recalls, "so we called a financial advisor, somebody whose name we had seen in a newspaper advertisement, and asked his advice."

The advisor pointed out that the Marks needed a source of steady income with some growth in their portfolio to account for inflation. He had them complete and sign a Know Your Client (KYC) form that identified the ideal combination of investments as 40 percent low-risk

---

*Pseudonyms. Based on a case study from the OBSI newsletter, *Contact*.

and 60 percent high-risk investments, which translated into a blend of bonds and mutual funds.

For six years, the Marks withdrew $1000 monthly from the portfolio before discovering that their portfolio was depleted by about $100,000 during a period of steady growth in the bond and stock market. This was about $30,000 more than the balance should have dropped even without earning any returns on the bonds, which did not make sense. When they confronted the advisor about the loss, he suggested they transfer their portfolio to a new asset-management service and resigned as their advisor.

Taking their complaints to the advisor's bank-owned brokerage, the Marks asked that their losses be replaced. The brokerage refused, claiming the investments had been appropriate and no compensation would be offered. When the brokerage's position hardened and it became clear they rejected the claim, the Marks took their case to OBSI (Ombudsman for Banking Services and Investments).

OBSI determined that the advisor's strategy of selecting low-risk and medium-risk investments for the Marks was reasonable, but the specific investments for the medium-risk portion were too high-risk. When challenged, the advisor claimed he had performed a correlation analysis to confirm the portfolio fell within the couple's risk tolerance limits but was unable to either produce a copy of the analysis or confirm that he had discussed it with the Marks.

After performing various calculations, OBSI proposed that the brokerage return almost $43,000 to the couple, less than half the amount the Marks had calculated counting the $30,000 depletion and the loss of anticipated earnings.

The Marks were fortunate. Thousands of other Canadians have lost greater portions of their investment portfolios under similar circumstances and received nothing in settlement. Many more Canadians lost a far larger proportion of their investments during the disastrous market drop of 2008–2009 and cannot hope to claim any settlement. The market rises, they will be lectured, and the market falls; you must be prepared to accept risk.

True, but isn't it as important to limit the risk of loss, especially for retirement portfolios, as it is to maximize the amount of growth? How can financial advisors explain losses of 50 to 60 percent in an overall market that dropped barely 37 percent in the same six-month period?*

When Canadians raise concerns over losses in their RRSP or RRIF that appear excessive, they're usually told markets are falling everywhere, and they have no reason to blame the advisor who shaped their portfolio.

This is unadulterated claptrap. One of the requirements of proper living quarters is to protect you and your possessions from the elements. Would you agree with an architect who suggested not incorporating a proper roof in your home because you'll always be comfortable in good weather anyway? Probably not. So why accept the investment industry's premise that they're only responsible for rising markets and can do little to assist you when they fall?

The investment industry needs to acknowledge that its role is to maintain stewardship over the portfolios under their management, a task that extends into rainy days as well as during sunny weather. The task includes paying sufficient attention to defensive strategies that will cushion the impact of extended market slumps on the assets of clients, especially those aged 50 and over.

Severe losses as a result of major market downturns can leave investors traumatized, persuading them to abandon the market entirely and restrict themselves to low-paying bank savings accounts or government bonds. That's understandable, but unfortunate. It's not a matter of abandoning the market as a means of building retirement security.

---

*May 30, 2008 (S&P/TSX 14,714.73), to November 30, 2008 (S&P/TSX 9,270.62).

It's a matter of being realistic about the way the market works, and dealing with it accordingly.

Many within the investment industry claim the idea of expecting financial advisors to spend as much effort preserving capital as they spend growing assets is unreasonable. And it may be, until Canadians acquire a minimum of investment knowledge and accept a reasonable degree of responsibility for their actions and decisions. Too many RRSP owners, for example, believed that the years of double-digit annual growth in asset values seen in the mid-1990s would extend ad infinitum, or at least until their retirement. This nonsense was rarely contradicted by promotion-conscious mutual funds or the commission-based advisors selling them, but it's a reality that anyone who reads the headlines of a newspaper can grasp.

The trick may be to look both up and down—up toward potential growth and down toward possible losses. Have you ever asked a financial advisor (or yourself), "What are we doing to protect at least a portion of my portfolio against major losses?" If you haven't, you should. And quickly.

There Are No Magic Cures in Health or in Finance

I've often imagined that somewhere, perhaps in a dusty subterranean vault off Bay Street, dwell people with names like Igor and Elvira who wear pointed hats and keep spiders for pets. I picture them scanning the business sections of newspapers, eavesdropping on telephone calls between investors, and scribbling notes about investor fears between sips of fermented bug juice. This, I figure, is how the industry comes up with ideas like principal protected notes (PPNs).

PPNs sound like one of those household gadgets sold on television at three in the morning. Whatever concern you have about life, love, and the whole damn thing, these products promise to cure it. In the case of PPNs, the promised cure addresses your fears that the money you had in your RRSP or other portfolio will be around two, five, or ten years from now.

That's a legitimate issue. In fact, it's the subject of this entire book. But before you rush out to load up on PPNs, please keep reading.

Principal protected notes, like segregated funds and deferred sales charges, exist primarily to generate wealth for the investment industry. Gee, maybe the small investors who buy them will make a few bucks too, but that's not the issue.

This is no Aladdin's lamp of riches; it's a parlour trick that makes you feel good while your pocket is being picked. Here's how it works:

PPNs guarantee that the money you invest in them will be available at the end of a contracted period, as long as 10 years. This is not a big deal; placing it into a bank savings account will achieve the same goal. Those marketing PPNs—which includes practically every bank, credit union, financial institution, and street-corner loan shark—add the extra appeal of potential earnings based on stock market performance.

You can't lose: If the market rises, you collect profits; if it tanks, your original investment is returned to you. Hey, is this a good deal or not?

It's not.

Here's what goes on inside a traditionally structured PPN, also known among folks who track these things as the "plain vanilla" flavour.

Suppose a three-year PPN appeals to you because you like the idea of a guaranteed full return on your initial investment and the prospect of profiting if the market does well. You hand over $10,000 and sign the deal.

The PPN issuer immediately spends $9000 of your investment on a provincial or federal government-guaranteed strip bond earning perhaps 3.5 percent annually. The remaining $1000 is invested in a sector of the stock market described in the package. At the end of the term, the $9000 strip bond has yielded about $1000 for a face value of $10,000, the guaranteed principal. Whatever happened to the remaining $1000 is irrelevant to the PPN issuer because the only promise in the deal—to return the original $10,000—has been fulfilled. The invested $1000 is like "mad money" you might take to a weekly poker or bingo game. If you win, that's fine. If you don't win, well, you took a shot, right?

If the PPN term is five years, the issuer would purchase $8500 in guaranteed strip bonds at a similar rate and put $1500 into the market. Five years later, the original $10,000 is back (in the bonds) and any earnings are added. In a 10-year term, only $7000 need be put into the bond, leaving $3000 for market investment.*

It may occur to you that you could do the same thing yourself. Preserving the principal for a fixed period in this manner employs precisely the same strategy proposed in Chapter 4: From Propagation to Preservation. Whatever is left after the bonds have been purchased goes into the market. If you can simultaneously walk and talk, you can perform this trick on your own.

"Ah," you say, "but a PPN is convenient." So is riding to the grocery store in a chauffeur-driven Rolls-Royce. How much convenience are you prepared to pay for? PPN convenience has made a lot of people wealthy in recent years. Unfortunately, few are investors like you.

A Nickel Here, a Dollar There ...

No industry is more adept at sliding money out of your pocket while making you feel good about it than folks in the investment business. These are the people, remember, who brought you DSCs, trailer fees, and wrap accounts, and they weren't going to miss a similar opportunity with PPNs.

---

*This assumes an effective bond yield of around 3 or 3.5 percent, which was a little high in mid-2009 but historically very low. The amount separated from the original investment and placed in the guaranteed bond would vary, determined by the available interest rate needed until the original principal was earned back in the contracted time frame.

Buried under that sheen of PPN security is a layer of fees. The fees are applied to the portion of your investment left over after the PPN issuer purchases the bond. The size and number of fees vary, but expect to find at least some of these methods of siphoning money from your pocket:

- **Sales commission.** You don't really expect something to be sold without a commission, do you? The commission will range from 3 to 5 percent of the amount you invest, taken off the top. If no front-end commission is charged, expect a heavy DSC applied over the term of the investment.

- **Trailer fees.** Is this sounding familiar? A full percentage may be deducted each year you hold the PPN and passed to the advisor/salesperson.

- **Start-up and administrative costs.** Another 1 or 2 percent off the top.

- **Management fees.** Also labelled program fees or administrative fees. The amount may vary widely, from 1.5 to 2 percent in the case of passively managed ("plain vanilla") versions; up to 2.5 percent for actively managed PPNs (see below); and even the classic "2-and-20" fees for hedge-fund managers, if this represents the underlying security—meaning 2 percent off the top each year plus 20 percent of any net profits earned.

- **Interest costs and currency hedges.** Covering charges incurred from handling your money.

- **Miscellaneous charges.** Various administration expenses.

Purchasing a PPN is like handing over a portion of your hard-earned cash for someone to fly to Vegas, play roulette, and, if they succeed in winning, returning any profit, after deducting their expenses, back to you.

The odds against you are raised when leveraged investments are involved. Instead of investing the $1000 equity portion of your plain vanilla PPN on a dollar-for-dollar basis, the issuers and managers may leverage it five to one, purchasing $5000 in investments rather than $1000, multiplying your profit potential five times. This involves an interest charge billed to you, plus substantial downside risk to match the upside opportunity.

Should the leveraged investment pay off, the PPN issuer garners a fair-sized chunk of the profit. If the investment tanks—and with a five-to-one leverage, a drop of 20 percent (one-fifth) in the value of the investment eliminates the entire position—so what? The strip bond/guaranteed element in the PPN earns enough money at maturity to hand you back your original investment. You haven't made money but the PPN issuer has. Is this a good deal? Do palm trees grow in Saskatoon?

"Well," you may muse, "at least I didn't lose money." Yes, you did.

From 2003 through the 2008–2009 economic crisis, Canada's annual inflation rate hovered around 2 percent. Should you purchase a 10-year PPN and expect inflation to remain at 2 percent annually during that period—a highly unlikely prospect—a simple 2 × 10 calculation reveals that every dollar you set aside today will be worth 20 percent less when the PPN matures. Unless the invested portion of the PPN generates a net profit equal to 20 percent of your total investment after all fees have been deducted (an even more unlikely prospect than Canada maintaining a 2 percent inflation rate), you don't break even, *you lose.* Even with a more common five- to seven-year PPN, you need from 10 to 14 percent net growth over the term just to counter inflation.

You can always cash in the PPN before the maturity date. Or sell it to some other sucker ... er, investor ... on a secondary market. Just take your money and go home, right?

Wrong again.

First, there is no secondary market you can count on. Some issuers may offer to assist you in dumping your PPN at face value, but most avoid any obligation. If no buyer shows up, the only option is to cash in your PPN, waive any claim to potential earnings, and pay an early discharge penalty from 5 to 7 percent of your original investment. You may not have to worry about that problem if the company issuing the PPN goes broke. That's not likely to happen if the issuer is a major bank or giant investment firm like Manulife. But they're not the only wagons peddling PPNs, and you should know that your PPN investment is not covered by the Canada Deposit Insurance Corporation (CDIC) nor guaranteed by the federal or provincial government. If you honestly believe a company large enough to manage and market PPNs is not likely to roll over and stop breathing, I have two words for you: Lehman Brothers.

Risk-free? Think again.

By early 2006, Canadians had dropped more than $7 billion into PPNs, believing the marketing hype that they couldn't lose. Eventually, financial commentators began pointing out that the new emperor of the investment kingdom had a serious wardrobe malfunction. Investing in PPNs, they suggested, was like breeding rocks: heavy work with little return. Canadian investors were being scammed, and something needed to be done about it.

Regulators responded with all the alacrity of a rusty drawbridge while PPN issuers kept busy applying new lipstick to old pigs. CIBC called their PPNs "structured notes," which at least sounded as though a degree of activity was involved. Others injected life into their PPNs with the delightful description, Constant Proportion Portfolio Insurance (CPPI). CPPI is like the magic ingredients that manufacturers of laundry detergents claim improve their product. You never know what it is or exactly what it does, but it sounds so impressive that it must do *something*.

With CPPI, the entire amount of a PPN is invested in the under-lying asset, and the value is monitored. If the investment value begins to sink, some of the money is shifted into guaranteed bonds. Should the value drop to a predetermined floor price, the entire equity portion is exchanged for bonds; the floor price is actually the amount needed to ensure that the initial investment will be around at maturity. CPPI, it was claimed, potentially maximized returns without the risk or expense of leveraging.

In reality, it made PPNs more complex, which made it more diffi-cult for investors to understand all the costs and risk implications riveted somewhere in the boilerplate of the PPN prospectus. Even there, among the literary equivalent of a Beethoven symphony played by a rap artist on a tin drum, PPN issuers were not required to disclose details about fees and penalties.

The Investment Dealers Association (IDA), now the Investment Industry Regulatory Organization of Canada (IIROC), was suitably unimpressed by PPNs in a report. "There is no guarantee that the investor will earn any positive returns on the original invest-ment," the report's authors wrote, adding, "If the customer redeems prior to maturity, he/she can realize real capital losses on the investment."*

By 2008, concerns about PPNs finally attracted the attention of government regulators, who set tighter rules about disclosure of fees, risks, redemption penalties, and other delights.

A concluding observation on PPNs: Instead of searching for a risk-free imagined-growth investment trick, set your own risk tolerance and find an investment solution to meet it.

Regulatory Analysis of Hedge Funds, Investment Dealers Association of Canada, May 2005, p. 13.

10

LISTEN UP, ALL YOU
BABY TURTLES!

Jim Roache is not the kind of man you successfully delude, especially when it comes to investment decisions. Born in Newfoundland of Irish stock, he graduated from business school before pursuing a journalism career that led him into federal government work. "The things I learned at business school," the 63-year-old comments in his Ottawa home, "turned me against investing in the stock market, because you don't know the inside stuff that the top people get from their social networks. So I stuck to bonds, GICs, and treasury bills, relying on the so-called miracle of compound interest."

He did fairly well with this strategy throughout his working life, backed by a policy of controlling debt and paying in cash. When a debilitating illness struck in his 50s, Roache turned to an acquaintance he had known for some time, employed by one of the major bank-owned brokerages, to watch over his portfolio. Despite Roache's instructions to choose conservative blue-chip investments, the advisor shifted much of the account into high-risk stocks. "He even had me in Bre-X," Roache recalls, referring to the infamous gold mine swindle that cost investors billions of dollars when it collapsed.

When Roache recovered from his illness well enough to examine his account, he was appalled at the losses. "I called this long-time member of my social circle," Roache says dryly, "to ask what the hell he was doing, and he hung up on me."

Trying to bully Roache didn't help the advisor. Roache found six other investors in the Ottawa area who had suffered major losses at the same brokerage. Together, they formed their own Group of Seven and hired a lawyer to press legal action. "That was harder than you may think," Roache points out. "The brokerages keep many of the best legal firms specializing in investment matters on retainer, so representing individual investors becomes a conflict of interest for them. But we finally found a law firm that would take our case."

It took five years for the case to work its way to a negotiated settlement. In the end, Roache received a few cents on the dollar from the brokerage; the advisor was penalized with a two-week suspension from trading and ordered to return ("disgorge") commissions earned from the trades conducted in Roache's account, followed by three years of close supervision.

Roache looks back on the event with sadness, not over the loss of money but the betrayal of trust. "Losing the money hurts, but losing trust you put in someone you felt you knew as a friend hurts even more, believe it or not," he says. Then he adds, "A friend of mine commented that enemies kill you from a distance with large swords, but friends can do the same thing with shorter blades because they're closer."

He adds another analogy, this one referring to baby boomers who have managed to acquire substantial assets over their working years and must decide what to do with their money at retirement. "They're like those baby turtles, right out of the egg in the sand," he suggests. "They've got to run across the beach and get into the water to survive. Meanwhile, they have seagulls picking them off from the air and lots of hungry fish in the water, where they think they'll be safe."

Retiring boomers, like the vulnerable baby turtles, Roache suggests, need to develop hard shells if they hope to survive.

Investors, especially those engaged in the activity on a part-time basis to generate retirement benefits, have always needed to avoid seagulls and sharks. The rule continues to apply, but the game is now a little different.

The world changed during the 2007–2009 economic crisis. That's not hyperbole, it's reality, and it may take several years before the depth and breadth of the changes are fully understood.

Wall Street will no longer operate like a gang of preadolescent kids in a locked candy store while the rest of us feed them cash through the mail slot. North American automotive giants General Motors and Chrysler will no longer assume that everything they assemble on four wheels will find a buyer. And Canadians will cease trusting that somewhere, sometime, they will earn financial security in their retirement years by investing a reasonable amount of their earnings in reasonably structured investments for a reasonable amount of time.

Either Canadian investors concerned about building a retirement nest egg must become more aware of investment basics and more attuned to managing the assets assigned to that role, or the investment industry must demonstrate new and hitherto obscure dedication to protecting client assets.

Deals, Details, and Downsides

The investment industry is responding to change with new versions of old tricks. Among the magic solutions you can expect to hear are schemes such as:

Segregated Mutual Funds

The deal. Slide your cash into a "seg" fund and 10 years from now, you can count on pulling at least 75 percent out, along with any gains acquired from the underlying investment. If your fund value exceeds your original investment at any time during the 10-year period, push a switch and SHAZAM! The new amount is locked in for another 10-year period.

The details. When markets were riding high in 2006–2007, it almost made sense to lock in prices, even with seg fund MERs as high as 3 percent. Not now. You're dealing with a 10-year commitment; cash out before the maturity date and expect to be hit with a major penalty. Seg funds suit some insurance needs (beneficiaries receive the full investment amount upon the fund owner's death) but few investment goals.

The downside. Why consider a seg fund when market prices are depressed? Unless you believe that the world is faced with 10 years of constant deflation (in which case, we should all prepare to reside in caves and live off roadkill), why lock in depressed market prices?

Leveraged Loans

The deal. Stock prices should rise over the next few years by 10 or 15 percent annually, but why settle for trivial profits? Why not multiply your potential upside two, three, five, even ten times with leverage?

The details. If you have $1000 to invest, you borrow $9000 from a bank or broker. Now you can buy $10,000 worth of a favoured stock or mutual fund. If the investment rises 10 percent over the next year, you double your original investment, instead of settling for a 10 percent gain of a paltry hundred bucks. Interest on the loan is paid out of potential profits.

The downside. Anybody here from AIG? They and other Wall Street wise guys were leveraging experts. Are you? If your 10-times leveraged deal falls 10 percent instead of rising 10 percent, wave your investment bye-bye, perhaps along with an upfront commission of 5 percent to your broker and interest on the money you borrowed for the leveraging.

High-Yield Bonds
The deal. Bonds are good for protecting your assets, but government-guaranteed bonds are paying zilch in interest. So let's buy bonds that pay a decent annual yield, like 7 percent or more.

The details. Write this on your bathroom mirror so you read it every morning: *There are no high returns without high risk.* Not before. Not now. Not ever. High-yield bonds are issued by corporations that need cash quickly and will pay well above standard rates to get it. (Do not confuse these with quality corporate bonds issued by blue-chip companies and paying perhaps 2 percent more than government bonds.)

The downside. Instead of "high-yield," think *junk*. The higher the yield promised, the more likely that the issuers will renege on interest payments, go bankrupt, or refuse to pay the bond's face value at maturity.

Lifecycle Funds
The deal. Why be concerned about balancing your portfolio between growth and security with sufficient amounts of both? You have better things to worry about, such as your golf game and the prospects for Middle East peace. Have your advisor plug a Lifecycle fund into your RRSP or RRIF. Lifecycle funds incorporate a mix of different assets with a fixed target date, usually the day you plan to retire. As the date approaches, the fund's asset mix places an emphasis on fixed income and cash.

The details. Uh … wasn't it the role of your advisor to help manage your portfolio and find ways to preserve capital? Isn't that why he/she is paid commissions and trailer fees?

The downside. You'll pay a premium for these funds, and you'll still be paying (via commissions and trailer fees) your advisor for doing nothing. That's at least one payment too many.

Magic Rules, Exotic Trades, and Foolish Moves

Here's the magic rule about protecting your retirement assets from severe drops in market value while still being positioned for growth: *There is no magic rule.* None of the devices listed above will do the job and ensure a good night's sleep, let alone positive results. Wrap accounts, PPNs, and segregated funds are very effective at making money for packagers and promoters, less so for buyers and investors.

The best solution remains a talented and dedicated financial advisor who demonstrates as much concern for growing and preserving your assets as for his or her own. Unless your portfolio is well into the seven-figure range, however, this kind of financial saviour remains something of fantasy.

Pointing out that markets go down as well as up is little consolation to mature owners of RRSPs who recently watched their assets drop 50 percent or more in value. Traditional risk-reducing tactics such as diversification and asset allocation proved effective in the past, but in 2008–2009, when nothing seemed to help, a few people began searching for new methods of dealing with bear markets. Among their suggestions was an idea that appeared to contradict the very notion of reducing risk, yet may hold promise for advisors knowledgeable enough to apply it and investors confident enough to trust it.

Broadly put, it's the use of derivatives, the same exotic, poorly understood devices blamed for much of the Wall Street machinations that triggered our current crisis. Derivatives—the term is based on the idea of deriving investment tools from regular day-trading—were created originally to serve as insurance against substantial losses, not as an alternate means of earning profits from the market. Profits are made by treating options as products to be bought and sold by speculators.

The two most common derivatives are *puts* and *calls*. A *put* gives you the right to sell a commodity or security (stocks, bonds) at a predetermined date and price, and a *call* conveys the right to buy a specific commodity or security under similar circumstances. Each option has a *maturity date*—the last day it can be exercised—and a *strike price* at which the sale or purchase can be made. The most important option for a prudent investor to exercise would be a put—an option (but not an obligation) to sell a position at an agreed-upon price on a fixed date.

Here's how it might work:

Your 100 shares of XYZ Corporation have done very well in the year since you purchased them at $50 per share. Today they are worth $80; you expect them to reach $100 when you plan to sell half and recover your original investment, holding the balance for future growth. But if they were to slip below $75 in price, you would like to bail out.

So you buy a put—an insurance premium that permits you to sell the shares if and when they reach $75 in price by the specified date. By selling at $75, you will have earned a profit, less the cost of the put, and prevented a substantial loss.

Using puts and calls to build and protect your assets is like choosing to fly instead of drive from Toronto to Winnipeg; it's a great idea, but don't plan on doing it without a pilot. Those who propose these strategies suggest the best solution would be for advisors and financial planners who are sufficiently adept at using them to incorporate the tools in managing their client accounts.

A nice idea, but it defies the axiom of investors never placing their money in an investment or, in this case, a tactic that they don't understand. With an appallingly low number of RRSP owners unable to distinguish a bond residual from a balanced fund, can we expect investors to grasp the mechanics of puts and calls?

Before you can focus on a strategy to preserve your capital, you need to ensure that you are applying the best tactics to build it in the first place. This means, for the most part, dispensing with foolish investment errors. Here are 10 of the most common. Check them over and slap your wrist for every one you admit to committing.

These Errors Are Foolish, So STOP Making Them!

1 **Putting all your money in one place.** When GM sought bankruptcy protection in the summer of 2009, the press interviewed people who had sunk their entire retirement savings into GM corporate bonds and lost everything. Interviewers said they were unlucky. Balderdash. They were dumb as planks. Never place more than 10 percent of your money in any single company or industry.

2 **Investing in things you don't understand.** Would you slide your money through a mail slot into a place you've never visited, occupied by someone you don't know, to be used for a purpose you're not aware of? If you don't understand the business you're investing in, or the security you're asked to purchase, you're doing the same thing.

3 **Keeping investments that give you insomnia.** If you worry too much about the future and quality of an investment, dump it now. Anything that keeps raising second thoughts about your decision is probably doing so for good reason.

4 **Ignoring the cost of your investment.** Two costs to watch: The MER and other expenses associated with underperforming mutual funds; and the lack of reasonable growth potential from locking your money into low-paying bonds, GICs or savings accounts on a long term.

5 **Falling in love with an investment.** Ever had an investment kiss you goodnight? Loving the company whose stock you own or the cute logo for the mutual fund you bought doesn't mean you should let it rob you blind with poor performance. When the time comes to sell, ignore your feelings and become a cold-hearted capitalist.

6 **Keeping multiple RRSP accounts.** A surprising number of people maintain several separate RRSP accounts at different banks, brokerages, or financial agencies. There is virtually no benefit to this. The exception: CDIC insurance limits of $100,000 on cash-based (meaning no mutual funds) deposits may justify maintaining different RRSP cash balances up to $100,000 in different institutions. Maintaining several RRSPs makes it difficult to measure your asset allocation. What's more, some financial institutions charge separate fees for each RRSP account. Having one RRSP versus multiple smaller ones gives you more clout, i.e., more attention from the advisor, and better service.

7 **Trying to time the market.** You can't do it and make a profit. You may think you can, but you can't. So don't try.

8 **Avoiding your homework.** Know what you're buying. If it's shares in a company, read the annual report and learn what the company does, how long they've been doing it, and how much money they claim to make. If it's a bond or other security, know the maturity date and yield. This material is, or should be, made available to you from your broker/advisor. Do not trust the internet for this kind of information.

9 **Chasing success.** By the time you realize the roller coaster is climbing the Big Hill and you buy a ticket on the ride, it's at the crest. From that point forward, the ride is likely to have you screaming in

terror and demanding to get off. Usually at the bottom. Base your investment decisions on other factors.

10 **Failing to understand risk.** It's the other side of the reward coin. The more you want of one, the more you'll receive of the other. Assuming it's not there, or ignoring both the danger and the opportunity it represents, leads to disaster.

11

Mythical Beasts That Gobble Your Assets and Real Ideas to Build and Protect Them

Among the legends of the Algonquin First Nations people, none was more terrifying than Wendego. According to the fable, Wendego lurked in the deepest, most remote forests of the land, emerging in mid-winter to devour men, women, and children, and satiate its endless taste for human flesh before withdrawing to the nether regions again with the arrival of spring. Stories of the ravenous beast were exchanged around campfires for generations, growing more bloodcurdling with every telling. Fortunate victims, it was said, died of fright at the mere sight of Wendego. Others were eaten alive by the beast.

Wendego represented cannibalism, brought on by waves of starvation among the Algonquin, and the tales were a warning against failing to prepare for years of poor harvest, bad hunting, and extended winter. Our modern Western society doesn't fear a beast prepared to wander into town, devouring whatever it takes to satisfy hunger. Instead, we have inflation.

Canadians, and people in the world's industrialized regions generally, have managed to avoid the worst aspects of inflation for almost 30 years, an unprecedented achievement. The concept of guaranteed bonds paying 18 percent annual interest and home mortgage rates rising past the 20 percent level appears incomprehensible today. But it happened, and a similar event is almost certain to happen, perhaps as soon as 2012.

Inflation will be one of the costs of bailing the world out from the 2008–2009 economic crisis. The simplest definition of inflation is "too much money chasing too few goods," driving up the prices of commodities and manufactured goods and later pulling interest rates, real estate values, and other critical components up as well. Massive government expenditures in Europe and North America in 2008 and 2009 flooded economies with cash. Most of it was used to fund near-insolvent businesses, especially financial and automotive. Soon, this money will begin driving consumers to purchase goods and services, generating excessive demand. At that point, Wendego emerges from the woods.

Governments have learned how to deal with inflation, and with the promise of new, more effective international co-operation on global economic policies, we can expect to see effective cures applied. These would include hiking interest rates, imposing wage and price controls, and perhaps even linking currency levels to a gold standard, which would prevent governments from manipulating currency values. Few cures are painless and free from side effects, however, and we would be wise to prepare ourselves for both the disease and its treatment.

For example, two things susceptible to serious damage by high inflation are cash and long-term bonds. While interest rates on savings accounts will be adjusted upward in inflationary times, they are not likely to keep pace with rising prices and the resulting devaluation of currency, and the result will be a net loss to account holders. Long-term bonds are also to be avoided; a 10-year guaranteed bond paying

6 percent annually sounded like a very good deal in 2009 when quality bond rates hovered between 2 and 3 percent. Should you buy one (assuming you could locate it, an unlikely event) with the plan of holding it to maturity, you would not be happy if and when inflation hits 10 percent or higher within a few years.

Stock market shares should rise at a similar rate with inflation but that's not always the case. High inflation affects business performance in various ways, few of them positive. One result could be stagflation, when interest rates rise along with unemployment levels while the value of real goods remains unchanged.

As with all crises, opportunities may emerge among the carnage. Long-term bonds purchased at the height of an inflation curve become highly attractive when the curve has passed.

A more likely opportunity lies with real-return bonds (RRBs) that deliver just what they suggest: interest adjusted upward year by year to account for inflation. The mechanics are a little complex, but the returns can be rewarding. Here are the calculations for a $10,000 RRB paying a nominal 3 percent interest encountering 5 percent inflation in the first year and 6 percent in the second year:

FIRST YEAR	
Principal	$10,000
Inflation	5%
Inflation Accrual (5% of $10,000)	$500
Principal at End of 1st Year	$10,500
Rate of Return	3%
Interest ($10,500 x 3%)	$315
Total Return	8.15%

SECOND YEAR	
Principal	$10,500
Inflation	6%
Inflation Accrual (6% of $10,500)	$630
Principal at End of 2nd Year	$11,130
Rate of Return	3%
Interest ($11,130 x 3%)	$333.90
Total Return	9.64%

In Canada, the federal government issues RRBs, providing the assurance of a government-backed guarantee along with inflation protection.

The principal drawback to RRBs concerns maturity dates. While a secondary market exists for the bonds, you may not be able to dispose of them as easily as guaranteed strip bonds from the same issuer if you want your cash back before the bond matures. And holding them outside a registered portfolio is not a good idea; the interest earned will be taxed annually at 100 percent (versus 50 percent for capital gains), making them best suited for RRSPs, RESPs, and RRIFs.

You could invest in a mutual fund dealing in RRBs, but most have an unacceptably high MER. One exception is the Real Return Bonds Index Fund from Barclays Canada, with an MER of just 0.35 percent. Still, if your horizon is long-term, owning the actual bonds may be a better choice.

RRBs represent an attractive method of building a fortress foundation for your RRSP to fight market meltdowns while offering inflation protection. Remember, however, that they are best held to maturity and may not prove liquid if you try to sell them at an earlier date. For that reason, keep a substantial portion of your bond position in more easily cashed strip bonds or laddered GICs. *Laddered* means a fifth of the GIC value matures in one year, another fifth in two years, and so on; every year another fifth (or 20 percent) of your GICs is cashed and another five-year GIC is purchased with the proceeds. It's an effective means of steadying wild fluctuations in GIC interest rates.

Building Blocks for Walls and Watchtowers

Let's review the materials needed to construct a fortress to protect our retirement savings plan from market meltdown while generating growth to counter inflation and improve our anticipated lifestyle in later years.

We begin with two basic ingredients: equities and fixed income investments. Together, they should represent 90 percent of your portfolio's total assets.

Until age 60 or 65, the percentage of your RRSP portfolio in fixed income investments should equal your age. These can consist of guaranteed strip bonds maturing in five years or less, and perhaps five-year laddered guaranteed income certificates (GICs).

Most or all of the strip bonds should be government guaranteed. You may want to purchase blue-chip corporate bonds to boost the lower government-guaranteed bonds, but these should probably not make up more than 20 percent of your total bond holdings.

Many investment commentators suggest extending the age-equals-percentage formula all the way to age 90, when RRSPs (converted to RRIFs at age 71) must be collapsed. That may be a little overly conservative, especially if you trust your judgment or that of an effective advisor to build a solid equity base. Bonds, remember, are for preservation, equities for escalation. You may want more asset growth opportunity from 65 to 80 than others; if so, keep your equities between 30 and 40 percent, assuming you've chosen carefully.

Should you reach age 80, you've beaten the actuarial odds. Along with this good news comes more good news: Annuities are now worth considering.

An annuity provides a fixed amount of income in exchange for a lump sum from the original beneficiary or *annuitant*. Hand over $100,000 or more from your RRSP or RRIF to a company providing the annuity (usually an insurance company) and it hands you back a cheque each month. The amount is fixed; once you do the deal, you can't change the payment. You can, however, choose among various options, such as a Joint and Last Survivor, the usual plan chosen by a married couple, which guarantees payments as long as one of the partners remains alive. Choosing an annuity with no guarantee means the monthly payments are higher but they cease at death. Men receive a larger annuity than women because their shorter lifespan means fewer projected payouts from the same initial investment.

Here are examples of the payments available for every $100,000 invested in a Single Life, Male, No Guarantee annuity as of June 2009. Note how the monthly payments vary widely among the insurance companies supplying the annuity:

COMPANY	AGE 60	AGE 65	AGE 70	AGE 75	AGE 80
A	$641.43	$700.85	$787.12	$890.48	$1023.98
B	$636.46	$691.43	$758.99	$842.62	$927.97
C	$601.43	$672.51	$763.39	$871.70	$985.09
D	$607.85	$694.87	$806.38	$950.15	N/A
E	$607.61	$712.70	$800.63	$938.49	N/A
F	$578.12	$647.22	$740.14	$867.24	$1040.46
G	$607.89	$673.22	$763.82	$891.96	$1077.05
H	$590.83	$668.60	$779.72	$936.45	$1144.74

As you can see, it pays to shop around. At age 60, the annuity (male, with no guarantee—once the annuitant dies the payments cease) yields as low as 7 percent annually ($578.12 × 12 = $6937.44) from company F. Hang on for 20 years and the same $100,000 brings you almost 14 percent annually from company H and barely 11 percent annually from company B. Two of the companies don't even want you to darken their door at age 80.

Summing up: Manage your RRSP/RRIF to age 80; pay attention to diversity, preservation of capital, and controlling costs and fees. At age 80, use all or most of your retirement assets to purchase an annuity (joint-survivor guaranteed is preferred, if you have a spouse or chosen beneficiary), collect cheques every month, and let others worry about wheeling and dealing.

Equity investments are still needed to generate asset growth from age 65 to 80. The U.S. investment industry dedicates enough effort in maintaining its records of performance to impress the most dedicated historian in the Vatican. It has tracked the annual returns on equity investments back to 1825, through the euphoric years, the disappointing years, the blah years, and the Oh-My-God! years.

For those investors who remain concerned about the potential for loss yet crave the opportunities for long-term growth, a breakdown of the 183 years between 1825 and 2007 reveals some encouraging facts:

- For 129 or 70 percent of those years, the markets produced positive growth.

- In five years—1862, 1879, 1885, 1933, and 1954—the markets scored between 50 and 60 percent growth. They have never fallen by a similar amount in any given year.

- For another five years—1843, 1863, 1928, 1935, and 1958— the markets delivered between 40 and 50 percent annual returns. In only one year—1931—did they fall that far.

- For a remarkable 15 years—including 1975, 1980, 1985, 1989, 1991, 1995, and 1997—the U.S. equity markets scored between 20 and 40 percent growth. They fell that far only in 1937.

- In over 84 of those 183 years, or 46 percent of the time, the American equity markets returned annual gains of 10 percent or better. In only 25 of these years, or less than 14 percent of the time, the markets lost 10 percent or more.*

If you're calculating odds, the chances appear better than 2 to 1 in any given year that you will post a gain rather than a loss from your equity investments. With this revelation comes the sobering insight that these performance figures are measured across the entire equity universe within the U.S., surely another argument for investing in broadly based index funds with minimal charges.

A few caveats are worth noting: Neither Dow Jones nor Standard & Poor's existed back in 1825, so the benchmarks employed in the early years (S&P dates back only to 1945) are unknown. And while today Canada's stock markets reflect most moves in the United States, this was not always the case prior to the Second World War, suggesting that a true parallel needn't apply.

Providing a Canadian viewpoint, Warren Baldwin, a Toronto-based financial planner, delved into files to report that bear markets occurring in the 50 years between 1958 and 2008 lasted about 14 months and prices bottomed out at a 25 percent loss. Bull markets, in contrast, lasted about 48 months and saw prices climb an average of 148 percent.

It's all a very convincing argument for staying in equity markets, assuming you are able to hold on to as many of your gains as possible in the face of unforeseen down markets and excessive fees and commissions.

---

*Value Square Asset Management, Yale University.

What of Allison Godden, who, as we saw in Chapter 5, abandoned equities entirely? Allison was converting past investments into fixed income. Growth in her retirement account balance was desirable but not as critical as 5 or 10 years ago.

From 1994 to 2009, Canadian equity markets, measured by the S&P/TSX, averaged an 8.60 percent annual return; Canadian fixed income investments averaged 6.06 percent annually. Extend the period from 1989 to 2009, and the gap narrows: 7.73 percent for equities and 6.70 percent for fixed income. The relatively small 1.03 percent difference over 20 years becomes significant with the impact of compound interest. Also, as we saw earlier, fixed income investments steady your account against volatility. Until age 80, it's still wise, however, to retain some quality equity investments.

Holding on to More of Your Money

The best solution remains ETFs invested in a broadly based index such as the S&P/TSX Composite. ETFs should represent 80 percent of your equity portion. The remaining 20 percent or less could be filled by dividend-paying shares of blue-chip domestic firms in industries such as finance (those sly money-making chartered banks), utilities (oil and gas pipelines are always busy), cash-rich consumer staples (Loblaws, George Weston, Couche-Tard—people have to eat), and health care (people also grow old). If you insist on adding a little spice to the mix, perhaps 5 percent could be in gold producers or emerging market funds, but expect volatility and remember to take profits from time to time. The following charts show examples using the traditional triage approach for age 60 to 71 RRSP investors.

Let's be clear: None of these portfolio models offers total protection against market meltdown. Each is a method of balancing growth against risk, and each can be easily tracked to assess growth and capital preservation. Each also can be assembled and held at minimum cost in commissions, management fees, and trailer fees.

CONSERVATIVE		
INVESTMENT TYPE	**GOAL**	**TOTAL ASSETS**
Money Market Fund or Savings Account	Cash for various needs	5%
Strip Bonds	Fixed income, preservation of capital	40%
Real Return Bonds	Fixed income, inflation protection	25%
Indexed ETFs	Growth	20%
Foreign Equity ETFs	Growth, international exposure	0%
	TOTAL	100%

MIDDLE OF THE ROAD		
INVESTMENT TYPE	**GOAL**	**TOTAL ASSETS**
Money Market Fund or Savings Account	Cash for various needs	5%
Strip Bonds	Fixed income, preservation of capital	30%
Real Return Bonds	Fixed income, inflation protection	25%
Indexed ETFs	Growth	30%
Foreign Equity, ETFs, Gold	Growth, inflation protection, international exposure	10%
	TOTAL	100%

AGGRESSIVE		
INVESTMENT TYPE	**GOAL**	**TOTAL ASSETS**
Money Market Fund or Savings Account	Cash for various needs	5%
Strip Bonds	Fixed income, preservation of capital	20%
Investment Grade		
Corporate Bonds	Fixed income, growth	20%
Real Return Bonds	Fixed income, inflation protection	5%
Shares in Domestic		
Blue-Chip Corporations	Growth	30%
Gold, Foreign Equity ETFs	Growth, international exposure, inflation protection	10%
	TOTAL	100%

Perhaps the Most Important Protection against Massive-Sized Losses: Good Investment Advice

The most outrageous falsehoods told by the investment industry to Canadians concern costs and risks. Too many financial advisors respond to client questions about mutual fund MERs, commissions, and trailer fees as though they are being queried about their sex lives. Someone should remind them, from time to time, about the ownership of the money they are intent on managing.

The industry's treatment of investment risk is just as outrageous. Yes, all investment involves risk. Risk, however, is not a cousin to the legendary Wendego, some hairy beast that emerges out of the darkness and defies any attempt to hold it at bay. Risk can be managed. It's done every day by untold thousands of specialists around the world, odd people who track pork belly futures and oceanic currents to measure the likelihood of bond defaults, and price them accordingly. On a more down-to-earth level, your own local bank or credit union branch assesses risk when granting you a personal loan or mortgage, as does your insurance company when pricing a policy on your home, car, or life.

Remember: *Risk can be managed.* The next financial advisor who shrugs at concerns over massive, unexpected equity losses suffered by a client by muttering, "Markets go down as well as up" and "All investment involves risk" deserves to be locked in a room for 24 hours and harangued with these words by a choir of economists bellowing through a PA system whose volume level is cranked up to 11.

Real Ideas You Can Begin Using Now

Time to summarize:

- **If you haven't opened an RRSP account yet, get started.** Now. You can no longer count on anyone but yourself to provide an adequate retirement income.

- **If you have an RRSP, keep contributing.** RRSPs are not perfect, but this is after all an imperfect world. From a tax situation, they represent the most attractive and least painful of all the practical alternatives.

- **Establish an investment strategy with your spouse and/or your financial advisor.** This may include establishing a balance between equity and fixed income investments; setting a goal to achieve in five years or at your presumed retirement date; choosing or rejecting investment sectors such as gold, foreign investments, emerging markets, and so on.

- **Limit the number of mutual funds in your portfolio.** Most investors do not need more than three or four: Two large-cap domestic equity funds, each with a different investing style (value stocks versus growth stocks and so on), an international equity fund, and perhaps a specialized fund investing in certain commodities or geographical areas. Or invest exclusively in ETFs (see below).

- **Investigate exchange traded funds (ETFs).** Think about placing at least one broadly based ETF reflecting the Canadian market generally, in your portfolio, plus perhaps 5 percent each in a global and an industrial sector fund.

- **Consider adding shares in selected blue-chip companies with a long record of paying dividends.** Among the candidates: Canadian chartered banks, pipeline and energy companies, large gold producers, large retailers.

- **Learn the cost of every investment in your portfolio.** The MER of mutual funds, commissions on common shares and bonds, administration fees, and so on.

- **Always know where your money is and how well your investments are performing.** Check your statements as soon as they arrive to (1) confirm that you authorized any transactions since the last statement; (2) compare the performance of your investments with the economic situation generally; and (c) note any subject you should raise in the next conversation with your financial advisor.

- **Avoid leveraged investments.** Your RRSP or RRIF doesn't need the risk.

- **Rebalance your portfolio from time to time.** Set a profit target for each investment. When it is achieved, sell a portion to crystallize your profits, perhaps investing the funds in strip bonds. Also, until age 65 at least, match the percentage of your portfolio in fixed and guaranteed investments (bonds, GICs) to your age.

- **Avoid investing in anything you do not adequately understand.** This rule should be inflexible.

- **Keep your guard up against fraudsters.** Not everyone you encounter who offers investment advice or opportunities is dishonest, but if they are crooked, you can't tell until it's too late.

- **Take pride in your independence and your ability to manage your financial future.** You may not have as much in your RRSP as you wish when you retire—few people do—but every penny in your plan is yours to own and control.

GLOSSARY

Accrued benefit The amount in an RRSP calculated as the contributions made together with any investment return (profit or loss) on the contributions.

Annuity A contract that guarantees a series of payments in exchange for a lump sum investment.

Asset Something of value. Your home is an asset (at least, the portion free of mortgage) as are your RRSP, RRIF, TFSA, and so on.

Asset allocation The percentage of assets invested in equities, bonds and short-term instruments (GICs, cash, and so on). These may be further broken down by region or industry sector.

Asset class There are three classes: equities, bonds, and short-term instruments. Each class has unique characteristics that influence its potential return and risk level.

Back-end load See *Deferred sales charge.*

Balanced fund A mutual fund that balances its portfolio risk and growth by including bonds and shares in varying proportions according to the fund manager's philosophy.

Bonds Cash loaned to a bond issuer, either a private company or government. The issuer pays regular interest over an agreed time before returning the full loan amount. Bonds can be bought and sold;

their price can fluctuate depending on interest rate expectations and perceived risk. They are relatively less volatile than equities with less growth potential.

Book value The value of net assets belonging to a company's share-holders, as stated on the balance sheet.

Callable Preferred shares or bonds that give the issuer an option to repurchase or "call" them at a stated price. Also known as "redeemable securities."

Capitalization The total amount of all securities, including bonds and common and preferred stock, issued by a company.

Churning The illegal practice of making multiple unnecessary trades in a client account for the purpose of generating commissions for the broker/advisor and the brokerage.

Common stock, or common shares A security representing ownership of a corporation's assets.

Coupon (bonds) Portions of a bond removed and submitted in return for earned interest.

Cumulative performance The gain or loss generated from an investment fund over a specified period of time.

Deferred sales charge (DSC) A fee levied on mutual fund investors who redeem their investment before a fixed period of time—usually five to seven years.

Defined benefit One of two ways to calculate pension benefits (see *Defined contribution*, below). A defined benefit is based on a formula incorporating years of service, salary history, staff grade, or other factors.

Defined contribution A benefit determined by the amount of contributions plus any investment return or interest earned.

Derivative A financial arrangement between two parties based on the performance of a security or asset.

Diversification Investment in a number of different securities, reducing risks. Diversification may be among types of securities, companies, industries, or geographic locations.

Dividend A per-share payment designated by a company's board of directors to be distributed among shareholders. For preferred shares, it is generally a fixed amount. For common shares, the dividend varies with the fortunes of the company and the amount of cash on hand.

Dollar cost averaging A method of buying shares or fund units with a fixed dollar amount on a regular schedule regardless of the price, lessening the risk of investing a large lump sum at the wrong time.

Equities Stocks or shares enabling investors to buy ownership in a company. Equities are responsive to market news in the short term, where their prices can rise and fall relatively sharply and quickly.

Exchange traded fund (ETF) Units of a mutual fund traded as though they were common shares.

Fixed income An asset paying a determined amount of interest for a specific period. Examples include bonds, GICs, and savings accounts.

Front-end load A sales charge levied on the purchase of mutual fund units.

Fund Any amount of money set aside for a particular purpose.

Growth stocks Shares of companies whose earnings are expected to increase at an above-average rate; their prices reflect investors' belief in their future earnings in growth rather than current or recent performance. The dot-com bubble of 1996–1999 was fuelled by growth stocks rather than *value stocks*.

Guaranteed investment certificate (GIC) A deposit instrument paying a predetermined rate of interest for a specified term, available from banks, trust companies, and other financial institutions.

Income funds Mutual funds that invest primarily in fixed income securities such as bonds, mortgages, and preferred shares to produce cash income for investors while preserving capital.

Index fund A mutual fund that matches its portfolio to a specific financial market index, duplicating the general performance of that market.

Inflation A condition of increasing prices. In Canada, inflation is generally measured by the consumer price index (CPI).

Interest Payments made by a borrower to a lender for the use of the lender's money.

Investment risk The risk that an investment's actual return will be lower than its expected return, including the possibility that it may lose market value.

Laddered A strategy for investing in debt instruments such as bonds and GICs. Typically, these are "laddered" over a five-year period by dividing the entire amount to be invested by fifths. One-fifth is invested in a one-year term, another fifth in a two-year term, and so on. At the end of one year, the invested amount plus interest is reinvested in a five-year term. The next year, when the two-year instrument matures, it is also used to purchase a five-year term. The instruments thus "roll over" and are reinvested every year. The advantage is to protect against sudden interest rate rises, which would weaken the value of long-term bonds while locking in good interest rates.

Leverage An investment that controls property of greater value than the cash invested, usually achieved through the use of borrowed money.

Liabilities All debts or amounts owing in the form of accounts payable, loans, mortgages, and long-term debts.

Life annuity An annuity under which payments are guaranteed for the life of the annuitant.

Lifecycle funds Diversified investment funds with different percentages of equities, bonds, and short-term instruments, adjusted over time to suit investors at different life stages.

Liquidity A measure of how quickly and easily an asset can be converted to cash.

Management expense ratio (MER) A measure of total level of expenses incurred by a mutual fund expressed as a percentage of the fund's *net asset value (NAV)*. Such costs may include transaction expenses, auditor fees, trustee fees, custody fees, accounting charges, printing costs, and other operational expenses.

Management fee The sum paid to a mutual fund's manager for supervising its portfolio and administering its operations.

Marginal tax rate The rate of tax on the last dollar of taxable income.

Market index A vehicle to denote trends in securities markets. The most popular in Canada is the Toronto Stock Exchange Composite Index (TSX).

Market price In the case of a security, the last reported price at which the stock or bond is sold.

Market timing The practice of switching among investments to profit from short-term market movements.

Maturity With a bond, the date at which it comes due and must be redeemed or paid off.

Money market A sector of the capital market where short-term obligations such as treasury bills and various commercial debt obligations are traded.

Money market fund A mutual fund investing in treasury bills and other low-risk, short-term investments.

Mutual fund An investment vehicle in which contributions by large numbers of small investors are pooled and invested by professional managers.

Net asset value per share (NAV) The total value of a mutual fund's portfolio, less liabilities, divided by the number of units owned by its investors.

Option The right or obligation to buy or sell a specific security at a specific price within a stipulated period of time.

Preferred share A share of a corporation with preferred claim on assets in case of liquidation and a specified annual dividend. Preferred shares do not normally including voting privileges.

Premium The amount by which a bond's selling price exceeds its face value.

Principal An individual's capital, or the face amount of a bond.

Principal protected notes (PPNs) A marketing instrument in which the investor is guaranteed to receive at least the original amount of the investment after a fixed term, plus any accrued profits.

Prospectus A document in which a corporation or other legal entity presents all legally required details relating to a new offering of securities.

Real return bonds Bonds that adjust the interest paid according to a defined means of measuring inflation.

Redeemable Preferred shares or bonds giving the issuing corporation an option to repurchase them at a stated price. Also known as *callable* securities.

Registered education savings plan (RESP) A plan enabling a contributor, on a tax deferral basis, to accumulate assets on behalf of a beneficiary to pay for post-secondary education.

Registered retirement income fund (RRIF) A maturity option available for RRSP assets, to provide a stream of income at the owner's retirement.

Registered retirement savings plan (RRSP) A plan to hold amounts deducted from taxable income, within limits, in a tax deferred state with various investment options and a tax deferral on investment income and gains. RRSPs must be collapsed—either redeemed for a taxable lump sum, converted to a RRIF, or used to purchase an annuity by the end of the year in which the holder turns 71 years of age.

Retained earnings The accumulated profits of a company.

Shares Documents signifying part ownership in a company.

Shareholders' equity The amount of a corporation's assets belonging to its shareholders (both common and preferred).

Short selling The sale of a security made in expectation of a decline in the price of a security, which would allow the investor to borrow, sell, then purchase the shares at a lower price in order to deliver the borrowed securities, pocketing the profit.

Simplified prospectus An abbreviated prospectus distributed by mutual funds to purchasers and potential purchasers of units or shares.

Strip bonds The capital portion of a bond from which the coupons have been stripped. The holder of the strip bond is entitled to its par value at maturity, but not the annual interest payments.

Term to 90 annuity An annuity that pays a fixed amount each year until it is exhausted in the year that the annuitant turns 90.

Trailer fee A commission paid annually to a financial advisor by a mutual fund company whose units the advisor has sold to clients.

Treasury bill (T-bill) Short-term government debt that pays no interest but is sold at a discount. The difference between the discount price and par value is the return earned by the investor.

Value stocks Shares of companies whose *book value*—the actual value of the company based on its range of liquidable assets such as property, equipment, inventory, cash on hand, and so on—is higher than the value of all of the company's outstanding shares, indicating it is under-priced. Investors hope to profit when the price returns to or above book value.

Volatility Extreme changes in the price of a security, varying more widely than the rest of the market; or extreme price changes over a short period of time in market prices generally.

Wrap account A prepared portfolio offered by investment dealers suppos-edly to reflect changing needs and expectations of the investor according to the investor's age and economic performance.

Yield Annual rate of return earned on investments, expressed as a percentage of the market price of the security.

Yield curve A graphic representation of the relationship among yields of similar bonds of differing maturities.

Yield to maturity The annual rate of return an investor would receive if a bond were held until maturity.

ACKNOWLEDGMENTS

Despite the dismissal by many members of the investment industry in Canada, a core of investor activists continue to grow and make their concerns known. They are a loosely knit group from varying backgrounds, many of them escapees from the industry they want to see subject to greater regulation. Their impact remains small—to its shame, Canada still lacks a national securities regulator, and our reputation for investigating abuses to investors and prosecuting villains is abysmal—but their numbers continue to grow.

I'm proud to count myself among this somewhat disorganized bunch and thank many of its members for their direct and indirect assistance in preparing this book. They include Stan Buell, Jon Chevreau, Larry Elford, Ken Kivenko, Gordon Pape, Jim Roache, Ellen Roseman, and Diane Urquhart. Gordon Pape would not likely include himself in this gang, but he remains a voice of wisdom and credibility worth heeding, as I do.

Preet Banerjee, Chris Cottier, Wendy Kormos, Gary Logan, and others who preferred anonymity were gracious and generous with their time—my thanks to them as well.

At Penguin, Diane Turbide's continued support for me is and always will be much appreciated. The editorial team of Helen Reeves and the constantly tolerant Sandra Tooze were a delight to work with, as was copy editor Heather Sangster.

And much kissing and purring to my home support team, Molly McGuire and my wife, Judy.

INDEX